A Young Actor's Scene Book

A Training Tool

edited by Barbara Marchant

The Scarecrow Press, Inc.
Lanham, Maryland, and London
2000

SCARECROW PRESS, INC.

Published in the United States of America
by Scarecrow Press, Inc.
4720 Boston Way, Lanham, Maryland 20706
www.scarecrowpress.com

4 Pleydell Gardens, Folkestone
Kent CT20 2DN, England

British Library Cataloguing in Publication Information Available

Library of Congress Cataloging-in-Publication Data

A young actor's scene book : a training tool / edited by Barbara Marchant.
 p. cm.
 Includes bibliographical references and index.
 ISBN 0-8108-3901-6 (alk. paper) — ISBN 0-8108-3902-4 (paper : alk. paper)
 1. Acting. 2. Monologues. 3. Drama—20th century. I. Marchant, Barbara, 1949-
 II. Title.
PN2080 .Y67 2000
808.82′45—dc21   00-056330

♾️™ The paper used in this publication meets the minimum requirements of
American National Standard for Information Sciences—Permanence of
Paper for Printed Library Materials, ANSI/NISO Z39.48-1992.
Manufactured in the United States of America.

To M. J. Marchant

There is a vitality, a life force, a
quickening that is translated through
you into action, and because there is
only one of you in all time, this
expression is unique. And if you
block it, it will never exist through
any other medium. . . . The world
will not have it. It is not your
business to determine how good it
is, nor how it compares with other
expressions; it is your business to
keep it yours clearly and directly, to
keep the channel open.

. . . You have to keep open and
aware directly to the urges that mo-
tivate you. Keep the channel open.
No artist is pleased. There is no satisfaction whatever at any time.
There is only a queer, divine dissat-
isfaction, a blessed unrest that
keeps us marching and makes us
more alive than the others.

Martha Graham to
Agnes DeMille

CONTENTS

Part 2: ADVANCED SCENES

One Female and One Male

Two Females

Part 3: LANGUAGE AND STYLE SCENES

One Female and One Male

Two Females

Two Males

FOREWORD

by William Esper

All acting teachers must continuously deal with the problem of finding scene material for their students.

It is an endless and time-consuming task because scenes that are used to train actors must meet very particular criteria. First of all, they must fall within the emotional ken of the student. Unless they can relate emotionally to the experience of the character, the enterprise is doomed before it is even begun. An actor can only create a truthful character if he is working in material that he intuitively understands. Without this connection, he will be like a traveler in a distant countryside who is without a map. He will stumble about and never find his way.

This is a particular problem for young actors in their late teens and early twenties. The teacher has to do a lot of searching to find material that is based on issues that young people can relate to and that has enough content to make it worthwhile for them and the teacher to work on.

The other issue that must be addressed is that the material must lie within the actor's technical grasp. To give a beginning actor, who should rightly be focused on fundamental things such as being in the moment, listening, and picking up on impulses, a scene that contains advanced character problems will not help that actor to grow. In fact, it will have a very destructive effect on him; it will confuse him because it will force him to concern himself with far too many things in one piece of work. One cannot see all sides of the moon at once, and one cannot work on every aspect of one's craft at the same time.

Barbara Marchant is a wonderful teacher with whom I have had the pleasure of working for many years. She has had extensive experience with young undergraduate actors. Now we can share some of her knowledge because she has generously given us a collection of scenes of particular use to teachers who work with young actors. The collection contains a wide variety of experience. In addition, she has helpfully arranged the scenes in categories for beginning and advanced students. She has also added a section of style and language scenes for those actors with the requisite skills to tackle them.

I believe that any acting teacher who works with young under-graduates will find this collection of scenes very helpful indeed.

ACKNOWLEDGMENTS

Thanks to the "Three Sisters": Sarah, Jessica, and Katie, David "Laverty" Schulman, Eva Mekler and Michael Shulman, Carol Thompson, Caroline Coughlin, Kevin Kittle, Joan Rosenfels, Vincent Murphy, Mary Ann Livingston, and special thanks to William Esper.

* * * * *

INTRODUCTION

We have all witnessed moments when a young actor gives himself or herself fully to the text. Those times when the work really comes together for a student can happen at many different stages of the training process, and they are unmistakable. The actor feels it. And as a teacher you know that the student has brought life, spontaneity, and truth to the work. It's what we all strive for.

In my experience such moments of truth don't happen by chance or luck or the gift of the gods. They are the result of the student's concentrated work in a program of systematic training, reinforced by text that is carefully chosen for each step of the process.

Since 1984 I've been extremely fortunate to work with undergraduate students in the Mason Gross Theater Arts Program at Rutgers University. During the sixteen years that I have taught in the intensive four-year program I have developed a system of training for young actors, and I have built up a huge library of plays for this age group. I have discovered that bringing young actors step-by-step to text is a powerful training tool that helps them develop their own unique instruments.

Developing this system of training for undergraduate students has been an evolutionary process. From the beginning my training with William Esper in the work of Sandford Meisner was the basis for my teaching philosophy. I knew that the first step was to help students get in touch with themselves and then to bring them in a logical progression to the material. I felt strongly that age-appropriate text was key to the process. It just wasn't right to put a nineteen- or twenty-year-old actor in a middle-aged role.

During my first years at Mason Gross, I spent months searching for material that was right for undergraduate students and testing it in the classroom. I learned what worked and what didn't work at each stage of the four years of training. I began to build up a comprehensive library of plays suitable for young actors. Through trial and error I developed a very clear system of when to give students each text. Some scenes I use year after year, and others I choose to help an individual student deal with a specific issue.

Over the years I've shared many of these texts with colleagues who also teach young actors. They, too, have used these scenes as training tools for their students. Now I am pleased to be able to share with you this selection of scenes for young actors. I have chosen the scenes in this volume for use in reinforcing curriculum for undergraduate actors, from freshman to senior year. It's a comprehensive selection that encompasses every step of the training process. Scenes range from very simple exercises to very advanced character work and can be used as training tools with any undergraduate acting program.

To give you a better understanding of my system, I'd like to give you a brief overview of our philosophy and our program at Mason Gross. Our philosophy is founded on the teaching principles of Sandford Meisner and William Esper. At Mason Gross we are dedicated to the principle that acting is an art. We believe that students must achieve technical mastery of their craft. We define acting as "doing truthfully under imaginary circumstances," and accept Sandy Meisner's principle that the "root of all acting is you." Thus our program is founded on the philosophy that technical skills must be firmly rooted in a tremendous sense of truth, spontaneity, and self.

Our four-year professional actors training program is designed to train young actors for the profession and is based on a systematic approach.

Starting from Square One

No matter how much experience a student has had, he or she must start at square one. This is the only way that they can break bad habits and begin to build a foundation that is rooted in truth. Two- and three-year-old children are spontaneous, truthful, and highly original. But as they grow older children begin to censor themselves and to respond from their heads, not their hearts. We want to get students out of their heads so they're not responding intellectually, but viscerally, spontaneously, and impulsively from themselves.

The First Two Years

In the first two years of training, students don't do any character work. It is so important at this time in their development for them to work within their own emotional range. At first some young actors don't understand why we don't allow them to act, but, in the first semester, they find how liberating it is to work spontaneously from their own responses. They begin looking at work with a greater sensibility for truth, and soon nobody complains about "not acting."

It's logical when you think about it. A ballet instructor would never assign *Swan Lake* to beginning students. First they'd start students at the bar, and then work them through a series of exercises, building one step at a time. That's exactly the way we approach acting — it's a step-by-step progression. On the first or second day of a beginning acting class, a teacher would never say, "Let's do a scene from *A Streetcar Named Desire.* You play Blanche, and you play Stanley." Students just don't have the tools at this point.

The entire first year, actors are learning about themselves and developing a responsive instrument. During the first semester students work with exercises designed to build their ability to craft and their ability to create imaginary circumstances and to live truthfully in the imaginary circumstances without the pressure of somebody else's words. We build from a very simple first assignment — five minutes of reality — to help them find a truthful, spontaneous, alive center.

In the second semester students begin text work, and the scenes are very simple and very close to their experience.

Sophomore year the work is much more emotionally demanding. The scenes are still contemporary, but we ask students to go much deeper emotionally. This year they also begin the first year of the Meisner training.

The Second Two Years

Junior year our students begin character work, which includes dialects, impediments, and heightened text. Now, they have to act, but by this stage of the process, they have developed a solid sense of truth so they are working from the inside, not externally.

Young actors often want to do material that is not appropriate for them at a particular stage of their learning. Because going too far beyond a student's emotional range can be harmful, teachers need to steer them to material that is right for them at that moment. A colleague who teaches in Manhattan had a student who wanted to do *Burn This.* She told him that it was bad for him at that time in his development and asked him to do *All My Sons.* He wasn't happy, but he followed her advice, and his performance was just bursting with life. She used text that was exactly right for him at that moment as a training tool, and he soared.

Senior year our students go to London for an intensive semester of British conservatory training in acting, stage, combat, historical dance, movement, speech, voice, dialect, and classical text. Although most colleges and universities offer programs abroad during the junior year, we feel that first semester of senior year is the right point in our training process for such programs. By this time students have developed a base that is deeply rooted in themselves. They are ready to take full advantage of the British training, which enlarges their capacity to play classical text, and gives them a competitive edge in the marketplace.

When they come back from London, they work on a senior project, and we get them ready for the business. They work on audition techniques, prepare monologues, and learn how to work on scripts for film and television, everything they need to know to enter the profession.

About the Scenes in This Volume

In this volume, I've chosen scenes that are appropriate for undergraduate students at every level, and I've divided them into Beginning, Advanced, and Language and Style material.

I've included a brief synopsis of the play and the scene setup as well as the text. Actors should always read the entire play from which the scene is taken. This will enable them to understand the character and the circumstances.

The Beginning Scenes Are for the First Two Years of the Program

These texts are appropriate for beginning acting students. The elements of these scenes are very familiar to eighteen- and nineteen-year-old actors in age, circumstance and language, so their first step into the imaginary world is a small one.

The Advanced Scenes Are for
Junior and Senior Years

These texts are appropriate for advanced acting students. These scenes are all character work and include the use of dialects, impediments, and heightened text.

The Style and Language Scenes Are for the
Senior Year

These texts deal with the particular challenges of period style and language.

How I Use Text as a Training Tool

These scenes follow the training curriculum at Mason Gross and track from freshman year to senior year. I've used each of these texts in my classroom, sometimes to reinforce what a student is learning. At other times I've used them to stretch a student or to have a student play against type. If students are in a beginning scene study class, I am very careful to pick material that's close to their experience. I've found that the key is to match the text to where they are in the training. Over the years I've seen students grow and develop as a result of this systematic approach to text and training.

I hope teachers will enjoy using this volume as a source book for scenes to reinforce undergraduate training and that students will find it useful in their ongoing quest to develop their unique acting instrument, their artistry, and to find those exhilarating moments of truth.

Part 1: BEGINNING SCENES

All My Sons

by Arthur Miller

The Play

During World War II the shipment of defective cylinder heads has caused the deaths of more than twenty combat fliers. Joe Keller, the manufacturer of the parts, was exonerated, but his partner, Herbert Deever, was convicted and sent to prison. Keller has two sons: Chris, who has returned home from combat to make a life for himself, and Larry, who has been missing in action for over three years. Chris soon expresses his love for his brother's former fiancée, Ann, who is George Deever's daughter. The dark secret of Joe Keller's crime is revealed, and the play ends with a tragic conclusion.

The Scene

Chris declares his love for Ann and confesses the difficulties of resuming life after being in combat. Ann professes her love and desire to be wed despite the resistance from the family.

CHRIS: *(Calling after him.)* Drink your tea, Casanova. *(He turns to* ANN.*)* Isn't he a great guy?
ANN: You're the only one I know who loves his parents!
CHRIS: I know. It went out of style, didn't it?
ANN: *(With a sudden touch of sadness.)* It's all right. It's a good thing. *(She looks about.)* You know? It's lovely here. The air is sweet.
CHRIS: *(Hopefully.)* You're not sorry you came?

3

ANN: Not sorry, no. But I'm . . . not going to stay . . .

CHRIS: Why?

ANN: In the first place, your mother as much as told me to go.

CHRIS: Well . . .

ANN: You saw that . . . and then you . . . you've been kind of . . .

CHRIS: What?

ANN: Well . . . kind of embarrassed ever since I got here.

CHRIS: The trouble is I planned on kind of sneaking up on you over a period of a week or so. But they take it for granted that we're all set.

ANN: I knew they would. Your mother anyway.

CHRIS: How did you know?

ANN: From *her* point of view, why else would I come?

CHRIS: Well . . . would you want to? *(ANN studies him.)* I guess you know this is why I asked you to come.

ANN: I guess this is why I came.

CHRIS: Ann, I love you. I love you a great deal. *(Finally.)* I love you. *(Pause. She waits.)* I have no imagination . . . that's all I know to tell you. (ANN, *waiting ready.*) I'm embarrassing you. I didn't want to tell it to you here. I wanted some place we'd never been; a place where we'd be brand new to each other. . . . You feel it's wrong here, don't you? This yard, this chair? I want you to be ready for me. I don't want to win you away from anything.

ANN: *(Putting her arms around him.)* Oh, Chris, I've been ready a long, long time!

CHRIS: Then he's gone forever. You're sure.

ANN: I almost got married two years ago.

CHRIS: . . . why didn't you?

ANN: You started to write to me . . . *(Slight pause.)*

CHRIS: You felt something that far back?

ANN: Every day since!

CHRIS: Ann, why didn't you let me know?

ANN: I was waiting for you, Chris. Till then you never wrote. And when you did, what did you say? You sure can be ambiguous, you know.

CHRIS: *(He looks toward house, then at her, trembling.)* Give me a kiss, Ann. Give me a . . . *(They kiss.)* God, I kissed you, Annie, I kissed Annie. How long, how long I've been waiting to kiss you!

ANN: I'll never forgive you. Why did you wait all these years? All I've done is sit and wonder if I was crazy for thinking of you.

CHRIS: Annie, we're going to live now! I'm going to make you so happy. *(He kisses her, but without their bodies touching.)*

ANN: *(A little embarrassed.)* Not like that you're not.

CHRIS: I kissed you . . .

ANN: Like Larry's brother. Do it like you, Chris. *(He breaks away from her abruptly.)* What is it, Chris?

CHRIS: Let's drive some place . . . I want to be alone with you.

ANN: No . . . what is it, Chris, your mother?

CHRIS: No . . . nothing like that . . .

ANN: Then what's wrong? . . . Even in your letters, there was something ashamed.

CHRIS: Yes. I suppose I have been. But it's going from me.

ANN: You've got to tell me —

CHRIS: I don't know how to start. *(He takes her hand. He speaks quietly, factually at first.)*

ANN: It wouldn't work this way. *(Slight pause.)*

CHRIS: It's all mixed up with so many other things . . . You remember, overseas, I was in command of a company?

ANN: Yeah, sure.

CHRIS: Well, I lost them.

ANN: How many?

CHRIS: Just about all.

ANN: Oh, gee!

CHRIS: It takes a little time to toss that off. Because they weren't just men. For instance, one time it'd been raining several days and this kid came to me, and gave me his last pair of dry socks. Put them in my pocket. That's only a little thing . . . but . . . that's the kind of guys I had. They didn't die; they killed themselves for each other. I mean that exactly; a little more selfish and they'd've been here today. And I got an idea — watching them go down. Everything was being destroyed, see, but it seemed to me that one new thing was made. A kind of . . . responsibility. Man for man. You understand me? — To show that, to bring that on to the earth again like some kind of a monument and everyone would feel it standing there, behind him, and it would make a difference to him. *(Pause.)* And then I came home and it was incredible. I . . . there was no meaning in it here; the whole thing to them was a kind of a — bus accident. I went to work with Dad, and that rat-race again. I felt . . . what you said . . . ashamed somehow. Because nobody was changed at all. It seemed to make suckers out of a lot of guys. I felt wrong to be alive, to open the bank-book, to drive the new car, to see the new refrigerator. I mean you can take those things out of a war, but when you drive that car you've got to know that it came out of the love a man can have for a man, you've got to be a little better because of that. Otherwise what you have is really loot, and there's blood on it. I didn't want to take any of it. And I guess that included you.

ANN: And you still feel that way?

CHRIS: I want you now, Annie.

ANN: Because you mustn't feel that way any more. Because you have a right to whatever you have. Everything, Chris, understand that? To me, too . . . And the money, there's nothing wrong in your money. Your father put hundreds of planes in the air, you should be proud. A man should be paid for that . . .

CHRIS: Oh Annie, Annie . . . I'm going to make a fortune for you!

(One Female and One Male)

Album

by David Rimmer

The Play

Divided into eight scenes that span their years at Martin Van Buren
High School, two teenaged couples struggle with their sexuality and
their impending adulthood. Set in the sixties, *Album* ranges from summer camp, to dormitory bedrooms, to the senior prom. The music of the
period — Bob Dylan, The Beatles, and The Beach Boys — serves as an
emotional anchor for the lives of the foursome. The importance of these
teenage years is emphasized as the play explores each character's problems and perils as they come of age.

The Scene

Boo and Trish consider themselves runaways. Boo has stolen his parents' car, and they are on their way to points unknown. They have
stopped to spend the night at the Paradise Motel. It's their first time
together in a motel.

> *2 A.M. A room at the Paradise Motel. Two beds coming out from
> the L. wall. Chair at R. wall. Cheap and drab, like a million motel
> rooms. Outside: darkest night, no stars, strange twisted trees.*

> *Entering from R., Boo crosses the stage, wearing his sunglasses,
> carrying a laundry bag, a guitar case, a copy of Sgt. Pepper.*

Opens the door with a key, turns on the light. Strolls into the room, chucks his stuff on the bed. Walks all around, smiling, checking everything out, taking it all in, digging it. Pulls out the Teachers' Room radio from his laundry bag, sets it down near the bed, plugs it in. Stands there looking at the room, his hands beating a nervous rhythm on his legs. Takes the sunglasses off. "Runaway" begins to fade out.

A hand and a suitcase appear at the window, and Trish climbs in, grumbling, stumbling. Boo goes to help her. She gets her balance.

TRISH: I love this room. It's like . . . Study Hall.

BOO: You should've seen the desk guy —

TRISH: — The desk guy just gave it to you? He didn't ask any questions?

BOO: Yeah, but I faked him out. There was this sign on the wall that said "Servicemen Welcome" so I told him I was visiting my father at the Army Base and he couldn't get leave and I had no place else to go, so . . .

TRISH: There's no Army Base around here.

BOO: He believed me. You should've seen this guy. He was bald, he looked just like the guy in *The Tingler,* you know, the one that drives his wife crazy by filling up the bathtub with blood —

TRISH: Shhh — Places like this give me the creeps.

BOO: You been to a lot of 'em?

TRISH: No. But did you ever see that movie *Psycho?*

BOO: Yeah. Four times. *(He suddenly does the shower-scene scream and comes after her like Tony Perkins. She screams and runs to the other side of the room. Dylan voice.)* Well whaddaya know, my mind ain't workin', I take a shower, I look just like Tony Perkins.

TRISH: Is there anybody else you like except Bob Dylan?

BOO: Winston Churchill. *(Laughs, jumps exuberantly on the bed. Sunglasses on.) This is so cool!* The Paradise Motel . . . First time I've ever been in a motel, first time I ever stole a car —

TRISH: — Your parents' —

BOO: — First time I ever ran away, first time —

TRISH: You have to keep saying that?

BOO: What? First time? *(Smiles.)*

TRISH: Don't look. *(She goes behind the closet door, taking the suitcase. He waits nervously, trying to be cool. He pulls down the bedspread, finds something on the sheet, flicks it away, arranges things neatly. Then he takes his guitar out of the case, and begins strumming and singing in Bob Dylan style the chorus of "Just Like a Woman.")*

BOO: *(Still strumming, makes the line part of the song.)* . . . Takin' that dress off, huh? . . . *(She comes out, wearing a pair of jeans and a loose-fitting peasant-type blouse, and holding on to her mother's album. He puts the guitar down, takes off the sunglasses and turns to her in anticipation. Disappointed.)* Oh, God what you got in there? You're holdin' it like it was Fort Knox —

TRISH: Nothin'.

BOO: You don't want me to see?

TRISH: If this place is so cool, how come they don't have a TV?

BOO: *(Hurt.)* Whaddaya think we're gonna do, watch TV all night?

TRISH: And the bathroom's down the hall?

BOO: What'd you expect, all the comforts of home?

TRISH: *(At the radio.)* I don't know why you had to steal this. I s'pose you think you're John Dillinger or somebody . . .

BOO: *(Little smile.)* John Dillinger? . . . It's possible. *(He starts prowling around the room; finds the Bible; leafs through it.)*

TRISH: What're you looking for?

BOO: Drugs. I thought somebody left some drugs in it.

TRISH: *In the Bible?*

BOO: Maybe a band stayed here. That's where they stay when they're on the road — motels. And that's where they hide their stuff — Bibles. They hollow 'em out — *(Heads for the closet.)*

TRISH: What would a band be doin' around here? Playing at the Army Base? You lookin' for drugs in the closet?

BOO: Found a dime.

TRISH: Great place for a band. I met a guy in a band once. He knew a guy who knew a guy who knew the Beatles —

BOO: *(Sunglasses on; Dylan voice.)* Ooooo, I'm impressed —

TRISH: He told me the original title of "Yesterday" was "Scrambled Eggs." *(She sings a couple of lines of the Beatles' "Yesterday," substituting "Scrambled Eggs" for "Yesterday." He tries to kiss her; she ducks. She picks up the copy of Sgt. Pepper.)* We can't

even play the album. That was dumb, you know, goin' up and gettin' this, you coulda got caught so easy.

BOO: I had to get the car keys, didn't I? What's the difference?

TRISH: The car keys were downstairs and the album was upstairs.

BOO: And my parents were asleep. Big deal.

TRISH: *(Reading the back of the album.)* I read the news today . . .

BOO: *(Sunglasses off.)* You know what was cool? When we first came
onto the highway, and seein' it stretch out like that, and then
takin' off . . .

TRISH: Yeah. The lights were nice.

BOO: . . . I kept seein' this vision of the car cracked up, right in the
middle of the highway. It was beautiful, kinda. You know, Dylan
had this motorcycle accident where he almost got killed —

TRISH: — That means we should do it too —

BOO: — And I kept takin' my hands off the wheel. Closin' my eyes
and driftin' like there was some kind of spell on me —

TRISH: Do me a favor, don't let me fall asleep next time I get in a car
with you.

BOO: I didn't do anything.

TRISH: Thanks!

BOO: You looked nice asleep.

TRISH: I wasn't just sleeping! You're not the only one who has *visions*
and all that stuff!

BOO: No — I know — I —

TRISH: I kept seeing myself in this big wheatfield in Kansas. And everything was in black and white. All the people, and the crows.
And the Scarecrow kept saying to me, "There's no place like
home, there's no place like home." We're not goin' to Kansas, are
we?

BOO: Nah . . .

TRISH: Good. We goin' to California?

BOO: I dunno. Maybe.

TRISH: Where *are* we goin'?

BOO: I dunno where we're goin,' we're just goin'! Okay? Trust me.

TRISH: Okay, maybe I'll just *go* to my graduation tomorrow.

BOO: What do you mean?

TRISH: I wanna go back.

BOO: We just got here!

TRISH: I don't care. I wanna go home.

BOO: I thought you hated it there.

TRISH: You think I want to live here? You think this is an improve-ment? *(He stalks around the room, pacing vehemently, ignoring her. She softens, tries to reach him.)* Hey, we don't have to run away.

BOO: Maybe *you* don't.

TRISH: You don't either. Look, our mothers and fathers are still gonna be our mothers and fathers if we run away or not!

BOO: *(Dylan. Sunglasses on.)* Not a chance!

TRISH: *Will you stop it?!* You're just hiding behind that!

BOO: *(Bitter.)* Hidin' from you.

TRISH: *(Quieter; reasonable.)* We can go back. Nobody'll know where we've been.

BOO: *(Anger bursting out.)* I want *everybody* to know where we've been!

TRISH: *(Angry back.)* Yeah if we have a "tragic accident" they'll know, they'll read it in the papers! "Two runaway teenagers killed in fiery crash" — that's what *you* want! —

BOO: That's what happened to James Dean and all those guys, and Dylan almost, I bet he wanted it to —

TRISH: That's the stupidest thing I've ever heard! You think I'm get-ting into a car with you again, you're crazy! I'd rather call my parents — I'd rather call the police —

BOO: *Police?* We're *criminals* now! —

TRISH: You're not *criminals* cause you steal your parents' car! —

BOO: *Shut up!! (She goes and sits on the bed, as far away from him as possible. Tense pause. He paces in small nervous circles. She watches him warily. He stops, looks at her, sits at the foot of the bed, trying to be gentle, taking his sunglasses off.)* Hey, I — *(She quickly takes the pillows from the bed and places them between him and her. Instantly enraged, he grabs them and flings them aside. She flinches and moves further away, cringing against the wall, reaching and grabbing for her photo album —)* What's in there, your baby pictures? (— *He grabs it, picks it up. She grabs for it, and they struggle. He pulls away with it and looks inside.)* Hey I remember this! —

TRISH: *(Furious; shocked; frightened.)* — What do you mean *you remember this??!!*

BOO: — You had all the Beach Boys songs in it —

TRISH: — You follow me home from school, you go through my drawers, you gonna put *Dragnet* on my trail next? You're worse than my mother!

BOO: *(Flipping through the pages.)* These're all Beatles songs —

TRISH: Give it back!

BOO: What's this? You write this?

TRISH: Don't read that! I don't want anybody to read that — ! *(She rushes up to him, but he fends her off.)*

BOO: What is it, your lovebook? Your diary? What'd you write — ?

TRISH: — *None of your business!*

BOO: *(He yanks it away from her, shoves her, holds it over the window as if to throw it out.)* Either I read it or nobody does — !

TRISH: *(Stumbling away; very emotional; feels beaten.)* Don't! It's my mother's!

BOO: I thought you hated her!

TRISH: *(Frustrated; confused.)* I — No, I — I wanna go home!

BOO: *(Angry; bitter.)* No place like home!

TRISH: *(Almost crying.) I wanna go!* I wanna see my dog . . .

BOO: *(Throws the photo album down.)* We haven't done anything yet!

TRISH: I'll die before I do anything with you!

BOO: *(Dylan voice: vicious, spits it out; sunglasses on.)* You told me — wanted to hold me — You just ain't that strong — *(Trish screams in frustration; yells back at him, her strength returning.)*

TRISH: I read the news today —

BOO: *(Wild insane Dylan; overlapping.)* Anybody can be like me —

TRISH: — A lucky man — made the grade —

BOO: — But nobody can be like you — luckily —

TRISH: — Blew his mind — the lights changed —

BOO: — How's it feel — you're on your own —

TRISH: *(Hands over her ears. Screaming.)* — Scrambled Eggs — Love's an easy game to play —

BOO: — No home — A ROLLING STONE!! —

TRISH: *(Chokes back gears of rage.)* STOP IT!! *(She suddenly runs to the door, fumbles with the handle, can't get it open, starts banging on it wildly —)*

BOO: Shut up! You'll wake the whole place up!

TRISH: I'll scream so loud I'll wake the whole world up! (— *He catches her, they struggle, he throws her roughly onto the bed. She scrambles up and stands at the head of the bed, like a cornered animal. He moves toward her to get her to shut up.*) Get away from me! — Don't come near me! — Help! *(Just as she screams, he rushes over and turns on the radio as loud as it can go. The loud instrumental part of the Beatles' "Good Morning Good Morning" blasts out.)* HELP!! I know why you did that — You did that so nobody'll hear me when you —

BOO: What? —

TRISH: — I've seen it in the movies, don't deny it —

BOO: — When I what — ?

TRISH: — *Don't deny it!* —

BOO: — *Deny what?* — *(He jumps onto the bed. They both stand there, hysterical, screaming at each other over the music.)*

BOO: WHEN I WHAT?	TRISH: DON'T YOU DARE!
DARE WHAT?	SHUT UP! YOU BETTER
WHAT'M I GONNA DO?	NOT —
WHAT? WHEN I WHAT?	I DON'T KNOW!
	I DON'T KNOW! *I DON'T KNOW!*

(He yanks the radio out of its socket and throws it down on the floor with a loud crash. She dissolves into tears.)

BOO: *Okay? Okay? (Still frustrated, he punches the wall, hurting his hand. Stops, turns to her, almost crying.)* What'd you think I was gonna do — ? *(He can't finish; breaks off with a sob; hides his face. She moves closer to him. He lifts his face slowly.)* I don't need any music. *(He kneels on the floor, beginning to break down. She kneels on the bed, getting nearer to him. His sunglasses have fallen off.)*

TRISH: You don't have to be Bob Dylan. You don't have to be anybody.

BOO: *(After a beat.)* We'll go home.

TRISH: Home? Never heard of it. *(She pulls him to her and hugs him. Then she gets up and turns off the light in the room. In the shadowy darkness, the Beatles' "Norwegian Wood" begins to play softly. They kiss, and as they fall softly back onto the bed, their kiss grows in desire.)*

SLOW FADE TO BLACK

All Summer Long
by Robert Anderson

The Play

All Summer Long, set in the rural Midwest, is a story about a crucial summer in the emotional development of the sensitive and confused eleven-year-old boy, Willie. Standing uneasily on the brink of adolescence and struggling to express himself in a distant and unappreciative home, Willie is championed and mentored by his disabled, older brother, Don. The two brothers undergo emotional experiences that affect them profoundly during this summer of family discontent.

The Scene

Ruth, Willie's older married sister, who cares only about her beauty and bitterly resents her pregnancy, witnessed Willie watching the birth of some puppies. Thinking that sex is dirty and sinful, Ruth berated Willie for watching the birth. Willie, ashamed of his behavior, has run away. Don, knowing the effect this will have on Willie's emotional development, wants Ruth to apologize to Willie.

The lights come up in the kitchen.
It is later that night.
RUTH *is in the kitchen, wearing a pretty bathrobe and is dancing with herself — just sort of swaying to the music of her portable radio — dancing as she can never dance with a man — a sort of*

15

pure narcissism. DON *comes from behind the house and up to the kitchen door. He stands at the door watching* RUTH. *He is obviously under a strain, but he is trying to keep himself reined in. He watches* RUTH *dance for a few moments, and then enters the kitchen.*

DON: You dance nice. My star pupil. *(*RUTH *puts her arms down and crosses to table, turns off radio.)* I don't understand you, Ruth. *(Crosses to screen door.)*
RUTH: *(Crosses to sink to pour coffee.)* Don't try. Any sign of Willie?
DON: No.
RUTH: *(Pours coffee.)* Harry and Dad are looking for him. He'll come back.
DON: Maybe.
RUTH: *(Crosses to down Left stool with coffee cup, sits.)* Don't look at me.
DON: Why did you talk like that? Why do you act like that? The sexiest girl in the neighborhood, and you're ashamed of sex.
RUTH: What do you know about it? You never heard boys snickering in school, on street-corners, looking at you — finding any excuse to handle you — dancing with you not to dance but to — What do you know about it?
DON: *(To up Center of table.)* Maybe not much. But I do know the way you talked to Willie was —
RUTH: Look, he'll come back.
DON: Maybe. But how?
RUTH: They'll find him — in the movies or someplace. Or he'll just walk in.
DON: *(Sits on up Center chair.)* I meant how — how? What kind of Willie's gonna come back?
RUTH: Jesus, you take on so — You'd think it was the end of the world.
DON: No, it's nothing as big as that, Ruth. But it is the end of something — the end of Willie as a boy — the end of innocence — the beginning of shame.
RUTH: Well, he should be ashamed.
DON: This was such an important summer for him, and I wanted it to be so good and so right. I wanted to protect him from all this cheapness. All summer, I tried — all summer long —
RUTH: *(Impatiently.)* Oh — *(She takes her cup of coffee and starts for the sink.* DON *sticks out his hand to stop her.)* Hey, watch out.

(She juggles the coffee cup to keep from spilling it, then puts it in sink.)

DON: *(Rises.)* I want to talk to you, Ruth.

RUTH: I'm tired. I want to go to bed.

DON: It won't take long.

RUTH: It's been a rough day.

DON: I know. But I've got to talk to you about Willie, and what you said to him this evening.

RUTH: Look, Mother's already talked to me. You can forget it.

DON: Maybe I can, but Willie's still going to ask me about it. He's going to ask me if what he did was wrong, and I'm going to tell him "No."

RUTH: *(Crosses, sits down Right chair, picking up cigarette on table.)* All right. All right.

DON: *(Follows her.)* And then he's going to ask me why you acted the way you did. And that's what I want to talk to you about, about what I'm going to tell him, when he asks me this.

RUTH: I don't care what you tell him.

DON: But, the only thing is, that now he's not going to believe what I tell him.

RUTH: And that kills you, doesn't it? To have him doubt what you say. To have him find out you can be wrong.

DON: But I'm not wrong, Ruthie, and you know it. And it'll have to be you that tells him, since you're the one that did it.

RUTH: *(Rises.)* You can tell him anything you want.

DON: *(Stopping her again by grabbing her arms.)* Look, Ruth, I don't like to talk like this, but this is important to me, and if you don't — I can tell Willie everything I know about you.

RUTH: Such as?

DON: I can tell him there's a child in your body and you hate it.

RUTH: You wouldn't!

DON: Why not?

RUTH: Let go!

DON: I can tell him how it was that night on the porch, and that it wasn't an accident that you hurt yourself on the fence. I can tell him what an ugly barren bitch you really are, and that he is never to be hurt by you, ever, and that he is only to pity you, as I pity you. (RUTH *slaps* DON. *After a moment, goes on.)* I can make it so that nothing you ever say or do to him after that could hurt him. I can tell him just once and get it over with.

RUTH: You wouldn't dare.

DON: The Hell I wouldn't. I'd do anything to keep that kid from being hurt by you, from getting your warped ideas on what's right and wrong, what's beautiful and what's ugly.

RUTH: You mean you'd do anything to get him back to believing that you're God Almighty on a throne.

DON: That isn't it, Ruth, and you know it.

RUTH: *(Crosses up to landing of stairs.)* I'll tell Mother. I'll tell her what you said.

DON: You tell Mother. And I'll tell Willie. And pretty soon there won't be anyone left for us to tell it to.

RUTH: You! You're the one that's going to tell them I'm ugly. Look at you. You're going to tell everybody. You! *(She tries to laugh.)*

DON: That's right. I'm the one.

RUTH: *(Coming down steps.)* Yes, you're the one. And I know why. Because you hate me. Because I'm a woman, and no woman will look at you any more. No woman would have you, and you hate me.

DON: I don't.

RUTH: You sit around all day doing nothing — nothing but reading books and telling Willie bad things. Damn you — damn you! *(She sinks on chair down Left of table and buries her head in her arms.)*

DON: *(After a few moments, with some compassion.)* Ruthie, whatever happened to you? You were such a nice kid.

RUTH: *(She turns the radio on.)* Nothing happened to me.

DON: I know you wanted to get away from here — that that's partly why you married Harry.

RUTH: We'll get away.

DON: I wanted to get away too — as badly as you did. And I was thrown back too — but that's all the more reason we should have made it so Willie wouldn't feel the same way we did.

RUTH: *(Rises, crosses to screen door.)* I don't want to talk about it.

DON: Sometimes I see you sitting on the porch, looking out into space, as though you were looking for the little girl who used to live here. (RUTH *says nothing. She is miserable. When* DON *sees that he is getting nowhere, he goes on quietly.)* One way or the other, I would like to feel that what happened today won't happen again. The best way would be if you would tell Willie yourself that you were wrong, worried about work, or something. Anything. Just that it was a mistake and that you're sorry. And after that you could just leave him alone.

RUTH: *(After a while she lifts her head.)* All right — I'll tell him.
DON: Good.
RUTH: When I see him, I'll tell him. But I don't believe it.

Boys' Life

by Howard Korder

The Play

Three former college buddies try to make their way with women and the big city. Cynical Jack, husband and father, pursues women by day while baby-sitting in the park. Phil, the most innocent of the three, concludes, after never being taken seriously by either gender, that being unhappy is the way things were meant to be. The handsome Don risks his relationship with his girlfriend by sleeping with yet another woman, just to see if he could get away with it.

The Scene

Lisa has just discovered a pair of panties in the bedroom of her boyfriend, Don. She confronts him about his latest infidelity.

> *(Lights up on* DON*'s room.* LISA *stands,* DON *sits on the edge of the bed. They are both in their underwear.* LISA *holds a pair of panties. Silence.)*

LISA: And that's all you have to say about it?
DON: What else do you want me to say?
LISA: How about sorry?
DON: Well, of course I'm sorry. How could I not be sorry?
LISA: You haven't *said* it.
DON: I'm sorry.

LISA: No you're not. *(Pause.)* I'm going. *(She starts gathering her clothes.)*

DON: Um —

LISA: What?

DON: I, ah —

LISA: YES? WHAT? WHAT IS IT?

DON: I just think you should realize that I've been under a lot of strain lately.

LISA: I see.

DON: And maybe, I've, you know, handled some things badly —

LISA: You're under a lot of strain so you go off and fuck somebody else.

DON: That's unnecessarily blunt.

LISA: Christ but you're a cheeky bastard. Couldn't you even bother to clean up before I came? Put away the odd pair of panties?

DON: I thought they were yours.

LISA: I don't buy my panties at *Job* Lot, Don. And I have a low opinion of people who do. *(She throws the panties at him. He fools with them and puts them over his head like a cap.)*

DON: They keep your ears warm.

LISA: You think I'm kidding, don't you? You think, well, Lisa's just having a little *episode,* it'll all blow over, chalk it up to boyish exuberance, hit the sack? Who the fuck do you think you are, James Bond? *(Pause.)* Did you use a condom?

DON: Huh?

LISA: A *condom.* You know what they are. You see them on TV all the time.

DON: Wha — why?

LISA: Because you slept with her, and then you slept with me, and you don't know who she's been fucking, do you, Don. DO YOU. *(Pause.)* I'm going.

DON: Where?

LISA: I'm going to lie down in traffic, Don. I'm going to let a cross-town bus roll over me because my life is meaningless since you betrayed me. I'm going to my *apartment,* you stupid shithead!

DON: Lisa, it was just a very casual thing. It's over.

LISA: What do I care?

DON: I made a mistake, I admit that, but . . .

LISA: But what?

DON: It made me realize something, something very important.

LISA: Yes?

DON: *(Very softly.)* I love you.

LISA: What? I can't hear you.

DON: I said I —

LISA: I *heard* what you said! "You love me"! That doesn't mean shit! This isn't high school, I'm wearing your *pin*. You want me to tell you what really counts? Out here with the graduates?

DON: What?

LISA: It's not worth it! Do what you want, it doesn't matter to me. I don't even know you, Don. After four months I don't know who you are or why you do what you do. You keep getting your dick stuck in things. What is that all about, anyway? Will someone please explain that to me? *(Pause.)* Don't look at me that way.

DON: What way?

LISA: Like a whipped dog. It's just pathetic.

DON: Lisa, please. I did something very stupid. I won't do it again.

LISA: Do you have any idea what you're saying?

DON: I'm saying I feel bad.

LISA: I'm sorry, but "I feel bad" isn't even in the running. Not at all. We're talking about faith. *Semper fidelis,* like the Marines. They don't leave people lying in foxholes. They just do it. They don't "feel bad."

DON: How do you know so much about the Marines?

LISA: It's not the Marines, Don. It's got nothing to do with the fucking Marines. It's the idea. *(Pause.)* You don't understand what I'm talking about, do you? You're just afraid of being punished. I'm not your *mother.* I don't spank. *(Pause.)* I'm going. Have fun fucking your bargain shopper and cracking jokes with your creepy friends.

DON: Lisa, wait, I have to tell you something.

LISA: No you don't.

DON: I had this dream about you last night.

LISA: How inconvenient.

DON: Can I tell you this? Just for a minute? Please? *(Pause.)*

LISA: *Start.*

DON: Okay . . . okay . . . now . . . I was . . . flying. In a plane, I mean, a rocket. It was a rocket ship. And I was all alone inside. With nothing to eat but junk food in rocks along the walls — sandwich cremes, Raisinets, boxes and boxes of crap. The smell was nauseating.

LISA: Does this go on much longer?

DON: Anyway I looked outside and there was this tiny planet floating by me like a blue Nerf ball. So I opened a bottle of Yoohoo and sat down to relax. But it must have been doped because it knocked me right out. When I woke up . . . the cabin was on fire! I tried to move but someone had tied me to the chair with piano wire, it was slicing into my wrists like they were chunks of ham. The ship was in a nosedive and I was slammed against the seat. Suddenly, bam, the whole port side blew away. I could see the planet rolling beneath me. A new world, Lisa. Pristine, unsullied. Virgin. I reached out . . . and the ship broke up around me in a sheet of flames. I was tied to a chair falling through the void. My mind left me. *(Pause.)* When I came to I was lying on a beach half buried in the sand. My right hand was gone. The wire had severed it at the wrist. Leeches sucked on the stump. I rolled over and waited for death. And then . . . you rose from the water on a bed of seaweed. On the white sands your hips swayed with an animal rhythm. I don't know why you were there. I didn't ask. You knelt down and gave me nectar from a gourd. You healed me in the shade of the trees. And you never spoke. And neither did I. I had forgotten how. Later on we built a shelter. You bore many children while I caught fish with a spear in the blue light of three moons. And then, one day, we lay ourselves down together on the sand. The breath eased from our bodies. And we died. And the ocean ate our bones. *(Pause.)*

LISA: What a crock of shit. You expect me to believe that?

DON: It's true. I dreamt it.

LISA: You've got a vivid imagination, I'll grant you that much. Very . . . charming. Very romantic.

DON: It's an omen. It's like a prophecy.

LISA: Of what?

DON: Of us. The two of us, together.

LISA: Well. *(Pause.)* You'd probably make me do the fishing.

DON: I wouldn't. I promise. *(Pause.)*

LISA: Wait. Wait. This is not it. This is nothing. I can't even talk to you until you tell me the truth. Why did you do this, Don? When you knew I trusted you? Was it her breasts, her buttocks, the smell of her sweat? Was it her underwear? Was it because she wasn't me? Did you have a reason? Any reason at all?

DON: I wanted to see . . . if I could get away with it.

LISA: Why?

DON: Because that's what a man would do. *(Pause.)* Let's get married, Lisa. I want to marry you. I want to be faithful to you forever. I want to put my head on your lap. Can I do that? I want to bury my face in your lap. I don't want to think about anything. Is that okay? *(Pause.)*

LISA: Would you like to play a little game, Don?

DON: What kind of game?

LISA: A pretend game. Let's pretend you could do anything you wanted to. And whatever you did, nobody could blame you for it. Not me or anyone else. You would be totally free. You wouldn't have to make promises and you wouldn't have to lie. All you would have to do is know how you feel. Just that. How would that be?

DON: I don't know.

LISA: Just pretend. What would you do? *(Pause.)*

DON: I think I would be . . . different?

LISA: Would you?

DON: I'd like to be.

LISA: Different how? *(Pause.)*

DON: Well . . . I would . . . I think I would . . . I think maybe I . . . *(He pauses and falls into a long silence. Blackout.)*

Hooters

by Ted Tally

The Play

Two nineteen-year-old young men, visiting Cape Cod for an adventure-some weekend, spot Ronda and Cheryl, two attractive girls. The pursuit begins. Cheryl is more interested in the eager young men, and the scene moves to a beach picnic, resulting in Clint "scoring" with Cheryl. His conquest, instead of fueling his macho image, shatters it, and Clint is suddenly confronted with a new understanding of himself and a valuable awareness of the ways of the world.

The Scene

Ronda and Ricky have been deserted by their respective best friends, Cheryl and Clint. Until the twosome returns from the motel, Ronda and Ricky are left in unpleasant company — each other's.

> *Saturday night. The beach. Bright moonlight. Surf. We see the wreckage of the picnic. RONDA is looking through the wadded wrapping paper in the basket. RICKY is sprawled some distance away, beside the cooler. He is sipping a fresh beer, and a small pile of empties has been neatly stacked beside him. CLINT and TRISH are nowhere in sight. RICKY watches RONDA in silence for a few moments.*

RICKY: May I ask you something?

RONDA: Sure love.

RICKY: What are you doing?

RONDA: What does it took like I'm doing?

RICKY: Rooting through the garbage, precious heart.

RONDA: It's called looking for something to eat.

RICKY: Don't you ever do anything besides eat?

RONDA: I *haven't* eaten yet. I'm still starving.

RICKY: No? What was dinner? What was that whole picnic I sat through, just a wonderful dream?

RONDA: Every single thing you brought was inedible. Honey.

RICKY: You're a real winner, you know that?

RONDA: Likewise! *(Silence.)*

RICKY: I don't *have* to sit here, you know. I don't have to sit around out here, if you really want to know the truth, just to watch you stuff your face.

RONDA: Don't do me any favors.

RICKY: I could drive off somewhere and get a burger or something. Play some miniature golf. Hang out.

RONDA: So drive! Golf! Hang, by all means! *(Silence.)*

RICKY: I *would* leave you here too, except I can't, because there's somebody I need to kill.

RONDA: With any luck you'll kill each other. I wouldn't want to miss that.

RICKY: That little asshole! How could he do this to me?

RONDA: Hey? *(Waves her arms.)* Hello? I'm out here too, you know. I'm the one who got stuck with *your* charming company.

RICKY: I don't even believe he could do this to me.

RONDA: What's to believe?

RICKY: It was my fucking plan!

RONDA: Well it's my fucking room they're in! Fucking!

RICKY: Don't remind me.

RONDA: Where am I supposed to sleep?

RICKY: Ask me if I care! *(Pause.)* I just don't believe this . . .

RONDA: I don't want to hear it again.

RICKY: You wait and wait —

RONDA: I said, I don't want to hear it!

RICKY: *(Pause.)* A weekend it's not raining, not too hot, not too crowded, not too —

RONDA: Shut up! *(She throws a plastic container at him, narrowly missing.)*

RICKY: Hey!

RONDA: What was that? That felt heavy!

RICKY: You vicious little —

RONDA: *(Stands.)* Give that back.

RICKY: *(Picks up container.)* No.

RONDA: *(Crossing to him.)* Give me that!

RICKY: No! You threw it at me. Anyway, I paid for it, whatever it is. *(Opens it.)* It's potato salad. *(Touches a finger to it, licks.)* No salt.

RONDA: *(Reaching.)* Give it to me.

RICKY: Get your hands off! *I'll* eat it.

RONDA: You're not hungry!

RICKY: I am now.

RONDA: You give me that! It's not fair!

RICKY: No, it's mine. *(She lunges. He pulls the container out of her reach and she falls against him. They wrestle and fall to the ground, then roll over it, fighting for the container.)*

RONDA: Don't drop it!

RICKY: Look out!

RONDA: You'll get sand in it! *(He manages to shove her violently away. She comes back at him, and he shoves her again. She slaps him, hard. He stares at her, astonished. Then be deliberately turns the opened container upside down and shoves it face-first into the sand. When she sees this, she bursts into tears of frustration and rage. He rises, watches her cry for a few moments, very uncomfortable.)*

RICKY: Jesus, all right! Take it, if it means so much to you. Here, I'm not hungry anymore.

RONDA: I hate you!

RICKY: Fine, good.

RONDA: I hate your lousy guts!

RICKY: Right, will you just take the potato salad?

RONDA: I don't want it anymore.

RICKY: You can pick the sand right off it. See? Here, I'll get you started.

RONDA: I wouldn't eat potato salad from you if it was the last potato salad in the world!

RICKY: Well it's not the last potato salad in the world, but it's the last potato salad on this beach and I wish you'd just eat it and shut off the goddam waterworks, okay? *(He crosses cautiously, puts it down beside her.)* I'm putting it down, okay? Right here beside you. Just a little sand on it, comes right off . . . . You'll eat it when you're hungry again. Jeez . . . *(He crosses back to his cooler, sits, takes out another beer and sips. During the following her crying abates, and she picks up the container. She brushes off the sand as best she can and eats.)* I bought a new shirt for this weekend, believe that? Look at it, it's torn, it's got crud all over it . . . all for this lousy weekend. *(Pause.)* You get a new shirt, you get Saturday off — which believe me, if you work for my old man is no picnic even if he is your old man. *(Pause.)* And you call up your former asshole best friend, even though you've hardly seen the stuckup sonofabitch all summer long since he got back from school, but hey — maybe he forgot your phone number! *(With rising anger.)* And you *collect* this asshole, and you cart him all the way up to Cape fucking Cod, *show* him this unbelievably great-looking chick, and *you* make the first move on her, *you* get her interested, you lay out your entire plan whereby you're going to make this chick, and then this. This! How does this make me feel?

RONDA: If that's supposed to be some kind of apology you'll have to do one hell of a lot better.

RICKY: I don't apologize to you! You clear on that? I don't owe you one goddam thing. *(Pause.)* I blame a lot of this on you, you know.

RONDA: On me?!

RICKY: On you, on you!

RONDA: How is that?

RICKY: She's your friend, you should teach her better manners.

RONDA: Since when is my friend my fault? I don't see you doing such a great job with your own lousy friend.

RICKY: That's different. I was betrayed.

RONDA: What was I? *(Furious.)* You think I would've even come here if it'd been my own idea? I came because she needed somebody to talk to. And then look what she does to me! And the worst thing is, the thing that makes me feel the dumbest, is that I *knew* she would. I swear to God, I think sometimes she can't even help herself! And you two! I sit here on this beach and I'm just some piece of driftwood or something, you're both talking over me, around me, through me — well I'd *rather* be betrayed! At least then somebody knows I'm breathing.

RICKY: *(Pause.)* You could've done *something* to make her stay.

RONDA: Did you even hear what I just said?

RICKY: Yeah, but you should've done something. *(Pause.)* How's your potato salad?

RONDA: Crunchy.

RICKY: Great. Wanna beer?

RONDA: Do you always drink like this?

RICKY: Like what?

RONDA: Into an alcoholic stupor?

RICKY: Whenever I get the chance.

RONDA: Charming.

RICKY: Jesus, you always gotta be such a hardass all the time?

RONDA: Have another one, little fella. You're still coherent.

RICKY: Don't you worry about my drinking, angel-drawers. I've drunk more beer than you ever saw.

RONDA: I'm sure you have.

RICKY: I've drunk more beer than you ever *heard* of.

RONDA: Land sakes.

RICKY: I can drink four quarts in one sitting — five!

RONDA: That must be quite a sight. You and Paul Newman in a chugging contest.

RICKY: Aw, just shut the hell up about Paul Newman, okay?

RONDA: Oh. I'm sorry. You probably thought we *believed* all that crap.

RICKY: *(Pause.)* I knew you didn't believe it. That was all part of the plan.

RONDA: Oh, I see.

RICKY: Chicks don't mind whether you're somebody important, long as you *act* like you are. Either get 'em impressed, or get 'em feeling sorry for you. Either way is good.

RONDA: Just make up some lie?

RICKY: Sure! The bigger the better. I once told this one chick I was about to become a priest, and she owed it to Jesus to test my spiritual purity one last time, see was I *worthy* or something.

RONDA: Sad to say, you flunked her test.

RICKY: Sad to say. But that's always a good one with dago chicks, you spot a crucifix or something. Or make it really outrageous. Like you were recently in this three-car pileup in the last lap of the Monaco Grand Prix and you've been paralyzed from the waist

down for three months. You've just now got out of intensive care
and you're starting to wonder whether you can still be a real man,
only you haven't met a chick you thought would really understand
and not laugh at you.

RONDA: Up till now, that is.

RICKY: See, you're catching on!

RONDA: And they actually *believe* this nonsense?

RICKY: Believe, what's to believe? Let me tell you something, and
you hang onto this as you go through life, because it's God's
truth. People will believe what they want to believe, and chicks
are no different.

RONDA: But what happens when they don't see any scars on your
body?

RICKY: They'll *imagine* them. Whatever! They *want* to believe it,
that's the point. If they don't they're still impressed you'd go to
all that trouble to bullshit them. Makes them feel really wanted.
You know, bullshit is the sincerest form of flattery.

RONDA: Aren't you a little worried about admitting all these top secrets to the enemy?

RICKY: What, to you? What difference does it make?

RONDA: *(She is stung; there's a pause.)* You've really done all this
stuff?

RICKY: Plenty of times.

RONDA: You're lying.

RICKY: I have!

RONDA: I don't believe you.

RICKY: So don't believe me. What the hey.

RONDA: I think you talk big.

RICKY: Screw you.

RONDA: I think you're scared.

RICKY: Of you?

RONDA: Of women.

RICKY: *Scared* of women?

RONDA: Yeah!

RICKY: No way. Absolutely no way. That's the theory it's convenient
for women to believe, a certain type of woman, but you got no
case. I like women. I idolize women — my whole life is built
around women! And women have always liked me too, and that's
no bullshit. Let me tell you something, one thing I am definitely

not is scared of women. *(Pause.)* Confused a little sometimes, *maybe.* Pissed off a little, okay.

RONDA: And I think scared.

RICKY: Well I think you're the one who's scared, sugartits. What do you say to that?

RONDA: Scared little boy. You live on big schemes and wet dreams.

RICKY: *(Pause.)* What about you, sister? What do *you* live on? *(Silence. She looks away.)*

RONDA: Look, are you gonna eat any of this potato salad, or what?

RICKY: I'm not hungry. *(He opens another beer and sips it, regarding her warily. Crossfade.)*

Love Allways

by Renee Taylor and Joseph Bologna

The Play

A collection of short plays about the foibles and follies of love and lovers.

The Scene

One of the 23 short plays, *The Love of Susan's Life* takes place in a bar where Susan is going to meet the newly found love of her life. Unfortunately, Mr. Right does not feel the same way about Susan.

SUSAN: Too complicated. *(At the seventh cutout.)*

MAN'S VOICE: *(O.S.)* I love you, I need you, you're the woman I have been waiting for for my whole life. Will you marry me?

SUSAN: *(Considers it.)* Too dull.

(Finally SHE *spots* NICKY *sitting alone at a table.)*

SUSAN: *(To audience, as* SHE *sighs, moonstruck.)* Mmmm . . . There he is. *(*SHE *sits next to him at the table.* SUSAN *puts her chin in her hand, rests her elbow on the table and looks at* NICKY *dreamily for a long moment.)* Nicky, I want you to know I love you. You're so perfect Nicky. Nicky, for the first time I know why I was born and my life has purpose and if anything ever happened to you, I would just die.

NICK: I don't know how to tell you this without hurting you.

SUSAN: You can tell me anything, Nicky. You won't hurt me. I love you too much.

NICK: I don't think I can see you tomorrow. I have to go to a wedding, and on Sunday my aunt's coming over and I . . . uh . . . have exams next week . . . and . . . uh . . . what I'm trying to tell you is I'm going to be pretty busy this winter and I think it would be best if we didn't see each other until the weather gets warmer.

(There's a pause. SHE stares at him.)

NICK: It's . . . uh . . . nothing permanent, Susan, but sometimes people need a rest from each other to go off and replenish themselves in new experiences and then if they decide they are happier with the other person, they come back stronger than ever and if they decide they are much happier without the other person, they still will always love that person for what they once had together. *(SHE stares at him with a frozen smile.)* I knew it would hurt you.

SUSAN: It didn't hurt me at all, Nicky.

NICK: That's good, Susan, I really have a lot of strong feelings for you.

SUSAN: It didn't hurt me because I didn't hear it.

NICK: Susan, try to understand. I think you're a terrific girl and I'll always love you . . . .

SUSAN: I heard that.

NICK: I'm not finished yet. I have strong feelings for you but I just don't think you're the girl for me and I want to end it before somebody gets hurt. So it's all over, Susan. It's all over.

(There's a long pause. SHE sits there with her frozen smile.)

SUSAN: *(In a painful whisper.)* There's a sharp pain from the center of my brain through my face and into my heart which feels cut up and the blood is gushing into my throat and I'm choking to death.

(There's a long pause.)

NICK: *(Sheepishly.)* Gee, I'm sorry to hear that, Susan. I wanted to break up with you still thinking I'm a terrific guy, but I guess that's too much to ask. Come on, I'll take you home.

(He starts to get up. SHE grabs his arm and starts squeezing.)

NICK: Susan, please let go of my arm.

(SHE continues to squeeze.)

NICK: Susan, you're hurting me.

SUSAN: *(Grabs him.)* Nicky, please don't go. Without you I'm nothing. If you walk out on me I might as well kiss my whole identity goodbye.

NICK: Susan, that's not a good selling point.

SUSAN: You love me, Nicky, you love me. You can't leave me!

NICK: There are just too many things about you that bother me.

SUSAN: What things, Nicky? Just tell me and I'll change them.

NICK: These are things you can't change.

SUSAN: Love moves mountains. I can change anything.

NICK: Your height. Can you change your height?

SUSAN: You don't like my height? I'm too short?

NICK: Too tall. I don't like walking with a girl who's that tall.

SUSAN: I understand, but I'm not really that tall, Nicky. I only give that impression because I feel tall when I'm with you. Look how short I am when I hunch over and stoop my shoulders. *(SHE stands in an awkward, unappealing position.)* Do you like me better this way, Nicky? I think you're right. I could look like this all the time. What else, Nicky?

NICK: Susan, please.

SUSAN: What else don't you like?

NICK: All right, your laugh. I don't like the way you laugh . . . "he-he-he."

SUSAN: I hate it too. He-he-he. I laugh with my mouth closed because I have a large bite. I'll see an orthodontist. I'll have my teeth filed and I'll laugh with my mouth wide open. Picture this with a smaller bite. Ha-ha-ha. See how easy it is to work things out. And we were so worried . . . Remember?

NICK: Susan, listen to me, there's more than that.

SUSAN: What, Nicky, tell me.

NICK: Susan, don't make me.

SUSAN: Please, Nicky.

NICK: Your personality.

SUSAN: What's wrong with my personality?

NICK: You don't have one.

SUSAN: I don't really think that's a problem, Nicky. I have no person-ality only because I thought you went for the helpless, wallflower type. I can change my personality . . . anything you want . . . moody, bubbly, effervescent, incoherent . . .

NICK: What about your brain? Can you change your brain? You're not smart enough for me.

SUSAN: Nicky, I've been holding myself back. I didn't want you to feel inferior to me. Ask me questions, Nicky. Go ahead . . . What's the capitol of North Dakota? Bismark! How much is 17 times 35? *(SHE starts figuring in her head and half aloud.)* Uh 17 times 30, that's . . . uh . . . ? Carry the 2 . . . that's . . . uh . . .

5 . . . no, 4. That's . . . uh . . . 2 hundred and . . . uh . . . no, 3 hundred; and 5 and 4 is nine, and 2 and 2, carry the one . . . that's . . . uh . . . 5 hundred and something . . . See, Nicky, you've never seen my brain?

NICK: *(Screaming.)* Have I seen your face and figure?

(There's a long pause.)

SUSAN: You don't like my face, or my figure?

(HE shakes his head.)

SUSAN: You don't think I'm pretty?

NICK: Sure, just not to me.

(SHE begins to cry.)

NICK: See. I wanted to end it amicably. I didn't want to hurt you but you made me say those things. Now I hope you're happy.

SUSAN: Nicky, if you don't like my face, my figure, my personality, my brain, or my height, then how can you love me?

NICK: *(Sighs deeply.)* That's the point, Susan.

SUSAN: *(Totally amazed.)* You don't love me?

NICK: *(Screaming.)* I can't stand you! How can I love you if I don't like your face, your figure, your personality, your brain, your height, your laugh, your bite, your walk, your clothes, your voice, your eyebrows and your watch!!!!

SUSAN: Why did you go out with me all this time if you don't love me?

NICK: I wanted to stop it in the beginning. But you see, I'm not perfect. I have one big flaw. I'm too nice.

(There's a long pause. SHE rises from her seat.)

SUSAN: Well then, that's it. Good-bye and farewell. And I mean it. Forever. You are the most despicable person I ever met. So, that's it. It's over. I loathe you and I'm really mad at you. You're a real crumb. So long and I mean so long, Hitler. You're a real meanie. So buenas noches, Mister, and . . .

NICK: For God's sake, will you get out of here and leave me alone?!!

SUSAN: I'll see you around, crumb! Hasta luego.

(SHE sticks her tongue out at him and leaves. There's a long pause, as NICK thinks.)

NICK: *(Remorsefully.)* I've lost her.

Sight Unseen

by Donald Margulies

The Play

Deep in the hype of the American art world stands the artist Jonathan Waxman. Shortly before Jonathan's work is presented at a London exhibition, he ventures off to the village where Patricia, archaeologist and former lover, lives with Nick, her British husband. Just as they spend their time as two archaeologists uncovering the past, so does Jonathan when he discovers a painting he had done of Patricia early on in their relationship. His feelings from the past surface into the present. Nick hates Jonathan and his art, while Patricia has never forgiven Jonathan for leaving her.

The Scene

Jonathan's mother has just died and the family is sitting shiva. Jonathan has gone up to his room to be by himself. Patricia, Jonathan's Christian girlfriend, comes to the Waxman home even though Jonathan has expressly asked her not to attend the funeral.

> *15 years earlier. Late afternoon. Spring. Blinds drawn. Jonathan's bedroom in his parents' house in Brooklyn, complete with the artifacts of a lower-middle-class boyhood, the notable exception being a sewing machine. Wearing a vest, suit trousers, and*

socks, Jonathan is curled up on a *bed. His hair is long. There is a tentative knock. Patricia enters. A beat. She whispers:*

PATRICIA: Jonathan? *(She waits, whispers again.)* Jonny? *(She looks around the room, gravitates toward the bookshelf, and begins scanning the titles. After a while, he sits up and sees her looking at a paperback.)* I love your little-boy handwriting. So round. The loopy "J" in "Jonathan," the "o," the "a"s. "This book belongs to Jonathan Waxman." *(Laughs, shows him the book.)* The Man From U.N.C.L.E. I wish I knew you then, Jonny. *(She returns the book to the shelf and continues looking.)*

JONATHAN: What are you doing?

PATRICIA: I love looking at people's books.

JONATHAN: *(Still awaiting a response.)* Patty . . . ?

PATRICIA: It's like looking into their brain or something. Everything they ever knew. Everything they ever touched. It's like archeology. Lets you into all the secret places.

JONATHAN: Patty, what are you doing here?

PATRICIA: Only took me two years to get in the front door. Hey, not bad. — Why isn't *Franny and Zooey* at your place?

JONATHAN: It is. I have doubles.

PATRICIA: Oh. *(Pause. They look at one another.)* You look handsome in your suit.

JONATHAN: *(He begins to put on his shoes.)* Thanks.

PATRICIA: I don't think I've ever seen you in a suit. Have I? I must have. Did you wear a suit at graduation? No, you wore a cap and gown. What did you wear underneath it? Anything?

JONATHAN: What time is it?

PATRICIA: I don't know. *(A beat.)* Your dad kissed me. When I came in? He kissed me. On the lips. He's very sweet, your dad. Said he was glad to see me, he was glad I came. See? He wasn't upset to see me. I told you you were overreacting. He's always kind of had a crush on me I think. *You* know the Waxman men and their shiksas. They're legend.

JONATHAN: *(Fixing his shirt.)* I should go back down.

PATRICIA: No. Why? Stay. *(She tries to touch his hair, he moves away. On his rebuff.)* So this is where you and Bobby grew up. *(She sits on a bed.)*

JONATHAN: That's right . . .

PATRICIA: Funny, it's just how I pictured it. Like one of those Smithsonian recreations? *You* know: those roped-off rooms? "Jonathan

Waxman's Bedroom in Brooklyn, Circa 1970." "The desk upon which he toiled over algebra." "The bed in which he had his first wet dream . . ."

JONATHAN: That one, actually.

PATRICIA: *(She smiles; a beat.)* I loved the oil painting bar mitzvah portraits of you and Bobby over the sofa by the way.

JONATHAN: What can I tell ya?

PATRICIA: Oh, they're great. *(A beat; She sees the incongruous sewing machine.)* Sewing machine?

JONATHAN: She moved it in when I moved out.

PATRICIA: Ah.

JONATHAN: The only woman on record to die of empty nest syndrome. *(She goes to him and hugs him.)*

PATRICIA: Oh, Jonny, I'm sorry . . .

JONATHAN: *(Trying to free himself.)* Yeah. You know, I really should go back down. My father . . . *(They kiss, again and again; he's bothered as her kisses become more fervent. Protesting.)* Patty . . . Patricia . . . *(She tries to undo his belt.)* Hey! What's the matter with you?

PATRICIA: Lie down.

JONATHAN: Patricia, my father is sitting shiva in the living room!

PATRICIA: Come on, Jonny . . .

JONATHAN: NO, I SAID! Are you crazy?! What the fuck is the matter with you?!

PATRICIA: You won't let me *do* anything for you.

JONATHAN: Is this supposed to cheer me up?!

PATRICIA: I want to *do* something.

JONATHAN: I don't want sex, Patricia.

PATRICIA: I've never known anyone who *died* before; tell me what I should do.

JONATHAN: This isn't *about* you. Do you understand that? This is *my* problem, *my* . . . loss, *mine*.

PATRICIA: But I'm your friend. Aren't I? I'm your lover, for God's sake. Two years, Jonathan . . .

JONATHAN: *(Over "for God's sake . . . ")* I thought we went *through* this . . .

PATRICIA: I want to be with you. I want to help you.

JONATHAN: You can't help me, Patty. I'm beyond help.

PATRICIA: Don't say that.

JONATHAN: It's true. I am beyond help right now. You can't help me. Your *blowjobs* can't help me.

PATRICIA: You don't know how I felt not being at the funeral.

JONATHAN: I'm sorry.

PATRICIA: No you're not. I was in agony. Really. I couldn't concentrate on anything all day. Knowing what you must've been going through? What kind of person do you think I am? I wanted to be with you so much.

JONATHAN: So you came over.

PATRICIA: You didn't say I couldn't. You said the funeral. I came over *after*.

JONATHAN: I meant the whole thing.

PATRICIA: What whole thing?

JONATHAN: The funeral, shiva . . .

PATRICIA: You mean I was supposed to keep away from you during all *this?*, like for a *week?* — isn't shiva like a week?

JONATHAN: Patty . . .

PATRICIA: Do you know how *ridiculous* this is? Don't you think you're taking this guilt thing a little too far? I mean, your mother is dead — I'm really really sorry, Jonny, really I am — and, okay, we know she wasn't exactly crazy about me . . .

JONATHAN: I'm so burnt out, Patty . . . My head is . . .

PATRICIA: *(Continuous.)* Not that I ever did anything to *offend* the woman personally or anything. I just happened to be born a certain persuasion, a certain incompatible persuasion, even though I'm an atheist and I don't give a damn *what re*ligion somebody happens to believe in. But did she even bother to get to know me, even a little bit?

JONATHAN: Oh, Patty, this is —

PATRICIA: It's like I was invisible. Do you know how it feels to be invisible?

JONATHAN: What do you think?, my mother's dying wish was keep that shiksa away from my funeral?! Come on, Patty! Grow up! Not everything is about *you*. I know that may be hard for you to believe, but not everything in the world —

PATRICIA: *(Over "in the world — ")* Oh, great.

JONATHAN: *(A beat.)* Let's face it, Patricia, things haven't exactly been good between us for months.

PATRICIA: What do you mean? Your mother's been *sick* for months. How can you make a statement like that?

JONATHAN: What, this is a surprise to you what I'm saying?

PATRICIA: Hasn't your mother been dying for months?

JONATHAN: I don't really have the strength for this right now.

PATRICIA: Hasn't she? So how can you judge how things have been between us? Her dying has been weighing over us, over both of us, for so long, it's colored so much . . .

JONATHAN: *(Over "it's colored so much . . .")* Look . . . if you *must* know —

PATRICIA: What.

JONATHAN: If you *must* know . . . *(A beat.) I* was the one who didn't want you there. It wasn't out of respect to my mother or my father or my grandmother, it was me. I didn't want to see you. I didn't want you there, Patty. I didn't want to have to hold *your* hand and comfort *you* because of how cruel my mother was to you, I didn't want that . . . I didn't want to have to deal with your display of —

PATRICIA: Dis*play?*

JONATHAN: Your display of love for me. Your concern. It was all about *you* whenever I thought about how it would be if you were with me! I didn't want you there, Patty. I'm sorry. *(A beat.)* I guess when something catastrophic like this happens . . . You get to thinking.

PATRICIA: Yes? Well? *(Pause.)*

JONATHAN: I don't love you, Patty. *(He smiles lamely and reaches for her as if to soothe her as she goes to get her bag. She groans, punches his arm, and goes. He stands alone for a long time before moving slowly over to the sewing machine. He clutches a pillow and gently rocks himself. As he begins to cry: lights fade to black.)*

Stanton's Garage

by Joan Ackermann

The Play

In a ramshackle garage miles from anywhere, two cars, both of which
were en route to a wedding, await repairs. One is Ron's, the ex-husband
of the bride-to-be, a man who missed his divorce and doesn't want to
miss his wife's wedding. A bridesmaid who is engaged to the best man
owns the other, a Volvo. She has her intended's teenage daughter,
Frannie, with her. They miss the wedding because the shop's mechanic
has never seen a Volvo, much less worked on one. Ron makes it to the
wedding but comes back to warn the Volvo owner that her fiancé is a
jerk. Meanwhile, Frannie falls in love with the amorous garage gofer,
Harlon.

The Scene

Frannie has offered to pierce Harlon's ear. They are very attracted to
each other and during the ritual of the ear piercing, fall in love.

> *It's 2:00 a.m.* FRANNIE *and* HARLON *enter with flashlight, a*
> *sleeping bag and a small paper bag.* HARLON *is dressed in his*
> *softball uniform and* FRANNIE *wears his cap. It's important in*
> *this scene that* HARLON *be ostensibly more nervous than*
> FRANNIE. *SHE appears to be experienced, worldly, a girl from*
> *the city.*

41

HARLON: *(Puts down sleeping bag.)* This here's your mattress. And . . . bed covers.

FRANNIE: Voila.

HARLON: You mind if I stay a minute or two?

FRANNIE: What do you mean, I'm going to do your ear, aren't I?

HARLON: I just didn't know if you'd mind me being in your bedroom. And all.

FRANNIE: It smells like manure.

HARLON: Mm. For Bonnie's tomatoes. She likes everything organic.

FRANNIE: Bonnie in Mexico?

HARLON: It's her garage. Inherited it from her daddy. Yeah, I've never been in a girl's bedroom before.

FRANNIE: Did she break the law?

HARLON: Broke a few laws. Broke a few hearts. There's a warrant out for her arrest.

FRANNIE: What did she do? Tell me.

HARLON: Six counts of fraud, for starters. Bait and switch. Regulation stuff. With the state, with her meters. Some woman sued her. Yeah, I've been in cars, movies, never a girl's bedroom.

FRANNIE: Why did the woman sue her?

HARLON: Bonnie sold her a set of tires she didn't need. Are you going with anyone?

FRANNIE: She sold her a set of tires she didn't need?

HARLON: Yeah, some New York bitch. Givin' Denny a hard time. 'Course Denny's too nice a guy to say anything.

FRANNIE: Were you honest with us?

HARLON: Huh?

FRANNIE: With Lee and me.

HARLON: Yeah.

FRANNIE: You honestly couldn't fix our car?

HARLON: Uh . . . we don't see too many Volvos.

FRANNIE: Well, I'm glad. I didn't want to go to that wedding.

HARLON: Good. I knew that. Silvie had it fixed within an hour, I pulled a few wires. Just kidding. Do you have a boyfriend?

FRANNIE: No. Look.

HARLON: What?

FRANNIE: The moon.

HARLON: You don't have a boyfriend?

FRANNIE: Look at it. Isn't it lovely? Do you know how to tell if the moon is waxing or waning?

HARLON: No.

FRANNIE: If the crescent is this way *(SHE describes the right half of the circumference of a circle.)* it's waxing, filling out this way. If the crescent is this way *(The left half of the circumference of a circle.)* it's waning. I can always tell what the moon is doing by how I feel. My favorite time to write is just before a full moon, I can stay up two nights in a row writing. Sometimes I can write on a waning moon, but my writing has a very different quality. Very spare.

HARLON: I never met anyone like you.

FRANNIE: Where's the ice? *(HE hands her ice in soda cup from the bag.)* Napkins? *(Wraps ice in napkin.)* Here. *(SHE puts it in his hand and puts his hand up to his ear.)*

HARLON: You smell good.

FRANNIE: I smell like manure. And mint. There's mint around here, too. You excited?

HARLON: Huh?

FRANNIE: Nervous?

HARLON: . . . yeah.

FRANNIE: *(Looking at the sky.)* Look at all those stars. Did you know that every atom in your body comes from a star? You have atoms in you, stardust atoms, that have memories you aren't even aware of; memories of events that happened in outer space.

HARLON: You sure you can do this?

FRANNIE: Do what?

HARLON: Pierce my ear.

FRANNIE: Sure. Matches?

(HE hands her matches. SHE lights a match to sterilize a needle.)

FRANNIE: You know how when people almost die, they see light at the end of a tunnel? They're just remembering their own light, from when they were a star. *(SHE studies the lit match, blows it out.)*

HARLON: Would you care for a Certs?

FRANNIE: No, thanks. How's that ice doing?

HARLON: Cold. So. You don't have a boyfriend.

FRANNIE: *(Touching his ear lobe.)* Can you feel this?

HARLON: Do it again. Yeah. I can feel it.

FRANNIE: We'll wait.

HARLON: Can I kiss you?

FRANNIE: No. *(Looking at the sky.)* Last month I watched the Pleiades passing through a day-old crescent moon. It was the most lovely romantic thing I've ever seen.

HARLON: You think that's romantic?

FRANNIE: Yes, I do.

HARLON: You think that's romantic?

FRANNIE: Yeah. What do you think is romantic?

HARLON: Kissing.

(Inside the garage, LEE, asleep, rolls over on the couch.)

FRANNIE: Shh!

HARLON: What?

FRANNIE: I thought I heard her moving, inside.

HARLON: She's gonna be your step-mother?

FRANNIE: That's the plan.

HARLON: Do you like her?

FRANNIE: She's okay. She's too paranoid. And wimpy, with my dad. Look!

HARLON: What?

FRANNIE: Look, a shooting star. Oh my God. Oh my God, look it's still going, it's still going, Jesus, it's still . . . it's still. . . it's still . . . oh. Wasn't that great?

HARLON: Yeah.

FRANNIE: I love shooting stars.

HARLON: I like them too. I don't think I like them as much as you do.
(Pause.)

FRANNIE: I love summer nights. Soft, warm, summer nights, just a little breeze. Crickets, cicadas. The smells — mint, manure, the linden tree, I even love the smells in the garage, the oil, the grease. It's heavenly. Celestial. *(Pause.)* You looked really good out there, in center field.

HARLON: Thanks.

FRANNIE: You made some really nice catches.

HARLON: Thanks.

FRANNIE: There was one I was sure you were going to miss, but you got it.

HARLON: Thanks.

FRANNIE: Can you feel this? *(Touches ear lobe.)*

HARLON: Do it again. Do it again. I don't think so. Do it again. No.

FRANNIE: Good. Ready?

HARLON: Uh . . .

FRANNIE: I've got the cork. *(Getting cork out of her pocket. SHE moves around in front of him, straddling him, her right knee up over his groin. SHE holds the cork up behind his right ear lobe.)* Okay. Let's fly this baby.

HARLON: You can leave your knee there.

FRANNIE: Here we go. You relaxed?

HARLON: You can leave your knee there.

FRANNIE: All right. I may not get all the way through in one go. But don't worry.

HARLON: 'kay.

FRANNIE: Here we go. *(Pause as* SHE *prepares.)* You're kind of moving around.

HARLON: 'kay.

FRANNIE: I have to get the right angle. I don't want the front hole to be higher than the back hole.

HARLON: 'kay.

FRANNIE: *(Pausing.)* This is harder than I thought it was going to be.

HARLON: *(Beginning to approach orgasm.)* Yeah?

FRANNIE: I'm not sure I can do this.

HARLON: Really?

FRANNIE: I'm afraid I'll hurt you.

HARLON: You won't hurt me.

FRANNIE: You're breathing awful hard. Try not to move around so much. Are you okay?

HARLON: Yeah.

FRANNIE: Okay. Here goes. Here goes. *(SHE jabs it.)* Did you feel that?

HARLON: . . . heard . . . it.

FRANNIE: It's not all the way through. You can't feel it? Can you feel it?

HARLON: Uh . . . .

FRANNIE: Try to hold still.

HARLON: 'kay.

FRANNIE: There.

HARLON: *(Climaxing.)* Ohh.

FRANNIE: You've got a hole in your ear.
   (Pause.)

FRANNIE: Can you hand me that napkin?
   (HE hands her napkin and SHE gets him to hold it against his ear. SHE gets off.)

FRANNIE: Did it hurt?

HARLON: No.

FRANNIE: It'll probably hurt a little when it thaws. You okay?

HARLON: Yeah.

FRANNIE: Sure? So. Now you've got a pierced ear. How's it feel?

HARLON: Good.

FRANNIE: You okay?

HARLON: Yup.

FRANNIE: You want the diamond stud or the little gold ball?

HARLON: The diamond.

FRANNIE: Good choice. *(Drops it.)* Oops, in the manure. Lee would have a heart attack over this whole procedure. Little spit. *(Putting it in.)* There. Listen to this little bit of carbon closely, you'll hear Wes from the dusty nebulas of space.

HARLON: No.

FRANNIE: No?

HARLON: When I listen to this diamond that I'll hear all the time 'cause it's in my ear, I'll hear your voice, Frannie. That's all. Your voice. And that's all I'll wanna hear.

(Pause.)

FRANNIE: Harlon?

HARLON: Yeah?

FRANNIE: You can kiss me if you want to.

HARLON: I do.

FRANNIE: I have to tell you, though.

HARLON: What?

FRANNIE: I'm not very clear about it. The mechanics.

HARLON: Huh?

FRANNIE: Should I hold my breath?

HARLON: You never did it before?

FRANNIE: No.

HARLON: You never did it before? You?

FRANNIE: *(Hitting him.)* Harlon, just tell me. What should I do?

HARLON: What should you do? Simple. Just . . .

(HE leans toward her slowly, kisses her tenderly, LIGHTS FADE.)

(One Female and One Male)

Voices from the High School

by Peter Dee

The Play

A collage of scenes depicting the complexities of coming of age in the high school environment.

The Scene

Stephen and Sheila appear to be sitting on a bench or a wall somewhere outside the vicinity of a high school.

STEPHEN: Coming new into this school isn't easy. If they don't know you here they can kill you. Like the first day I arrived I was wearing the wrong kind of jacket. Man, I couldn't have picked a worse one. I like how it looked on me in the store. I like material that shines. So I see this one kid staring at me and this leads to other kids seeing me looking at him staring and so I say: "Something bothering you, faggot?" And lucky for me I won the fight.

SHEILA: Did you hurt him?

STEPHEN: I don't know. I went crazy when I thought he bloodied my nose.

SHEILA: Did he?

STEPHEN: A little.

SHEILA: Like animals.

STEPHEN: Girls don't have to fight.

SHEILA: Oh yeah.

STEPHEN: Not like the guys.

SHEILA: Worse.

STEPHEN: In school here?

SHEILA: I don't care if anyone likes me in this school. Being new doesn't bother me. You don't have to be nice. I don't care.

STEPHEN: They beat you up?

SHEILA: Look, I don't need a protector.

STEPHEN: Who beat you up?

SHEILA: No one!

STEPHEN: You were crying.

SHEILA: I was not! Leave me alone. I didn't ask you to sit down here with me.

STEPHEN: Okay. Just give me a minute to sort of . . . drift off or they'll think *I* beat you.

SHEILA: Let them think what they want!

STEPHEN: Stop yelling, Sheila.

SHEILA: You don't know my name.

STEPHEN: It's not Sheila?

SHEILA: Yes. But I never told you.

STEPHEN: I'm Stephen. Hi.

SHEILA: I know your name.

STEPHEN: What's yours?

SHEILA: Nobody beat me up. I'm okay.

STEPHEN: I always think somebody's been punched out when I see 'em crying.

SHEILA: I wasn't crying.

STEPHEN: You got a weird eye problem then.

SHEILA: I'm okay now.

STEPHEN: Okay.

SHEILA: You can go.

STEPHEN: I am. *(Pause.)* Where you from?

SHEILA: Look . . .

STEPHEN: Where?

SHEILA: Small town.

STEPHEN: What made you move here? *(Silence.)* Huh?

SHEILA: My father got a new job after . . .

STEPHEN: What?

SHEILA: Nothing.

STEPHEN: It's not a bad jungle here. Lot of concrete you know.

SHEILA: Yeah. There was a . . . pond in the middle of the town square where I lived.

STEPHEN: Sounds pretty.

SHEILA: There were three silver elephants in the middle of it.

STEPHEN: Doing what?

SHEILA: Nothing much. Where'd you live before here?

STEPHEN: I've lived here all my life.

SHEILA: You said the first day you arrived you were wearing the wrong kind of jacket.

STEPHEN: Lived in a small town like you.

SHEILA: Yeah?

STEPHEN: Um hmm.

SHEILA: Why'd your family move?

STEPHEN: Family didn't. Just me.

SHEILA: Oh.

STEPHEN: They see me as the independent type. Just an aunt and uncle anyway, not really a family.

SHEILA: Who do you live with?

STEPHEN: 'Nother aunt. You're looking better.

SHEILA: I told you I'm okay.

STEPHEN: So what's your name anyway?

SHEILA: Sheila.

STEPHEN: You got a nice smile. Do you like ice cream?

SHEILA: You do this to all the new girls in school?

STEPHEN: Nope. This week's special is Jasmine Mocha Night.

SHEILA: I like vanilla.

STEPHEN: Come on. I'll treat.

SHEILA: No thanks.

STEPHEN: Hey, I'm loaded. I just knocked off that new guy from Jersey.

SHEILA: *(Laughs.)* You did not.

STEPHEN: Wait'll you taste their vanilla, it's the greatest. Let's go. Okay?

SHEILA: Okay.

* * * * *

The Scene

Patti is sitting in her room doing nothing. Bo, an older teenage boy, comes into her room.

BO: Hi, Patti. *(She looks at him.)* Your mother let me in.
PATTI: Uh huh.
BO: You haven't been to school all week.
PATTI: Right.
BO: Just thought I'd see you there.
PATTI: What's going on is that my mother called you, right.
BO: I missed you at school.
PATTI: She called you, right.
BO: I was coming over anyway.
PATTI: For what?
BO: What do you think?
PATTI: I'm okay.
BO: That's not what I hear.
PATTI: Well, it's what I know. And I'm the one who ought to know, right. I don't care what my mother's been telling you.
BO: She says you haven't eaten for too long a time.
PATTI: I'm not hungry. I don't want another person telling me I ought to eat. My mother's been in with that boring news. She's sent in my father who's not hungry either but who's chewing on automatic and now she's dragging you in.
BO: I called up to see how you were. Your mother didn't tell me anything; the way she was talking did.
PATTI: I'm not hungry. And I'd like to be by myself if you don't mind.
BO: For another week?
PATTI: For as long as I want.
BO: In this room not going anywhere?
PATTI: Quit hassling me!
BO: I'm not.
PATTI: Yes you are. *(Pause.)* You are.
BO: Can I sit down?
PATTI: Are you going to try to feed me?
BO: No.
PATTI: Sit. *(BO sits. They're quiet for a while.)*
BO: So.
PATTI: What?
BO: What have you been thinking about?

PATTI: Bo, did you come here to be stupid?

BO: No.

PATTI: I've been trying not to think about anything.

BO: Have you been successful?

PATTI: Bo.

BO: So tell me.

PATTI: Tell you what?

BO: What's got you in prison up here?

PATTI: I'd think that would be obvious to you.

BO: It happened to the rest of us too, Patti.

PATTI: The rest of you are the rest of you. I'm me and I'm working it out my own way.

BO: How are you working it out?

PATTI: I'm not just going to cry and moan and then wipe my nose and go on like it never happened.

BO: You think that's what we're doing?

PATTI: I don't care what any of you are doing. I'm not thinking about any of you. I can't.

BO: What are you thinking about?

PATTI: Carbon monoxide.

BO: Yeah?

PATTI: Surprised?

BO: Not a bit.

PATTI: I looked it up in a dictionary. Got the definition locked in my memory now.

BO: Tell me.

PATTI: "Carbon monoxide. Chem . . ." That's an abbreviation for chemical.

BO: Got it.

PATTI: "A colorless, odorless gas, CO, formed by the incomplete oxidation of carbon. It burns with a blue flame to form carbon dioxide, and is highly poisonous when inhaled, since it combines with the hemoglobin of the blood to the exclusion of oxygen."
    (Long pause.)

BO: Burns with a blue flame, huh?

PATTI: That's what the book says.

BO: Weird.

PATTI: Me?

BO: No, no . . . that phrase. That phrase that's all. It's just weird.

PATTI: "Burns with a blue flame?"

BO: Yeah.

PATTI: Why?

BO: Forget it.

PATTI: Tell me.

BO: It's sad. We've had enough sad shit. Look at you. You can't even get out of your room.

PATTI: Tell me, Bo.

BO: Why? So you can memorize it. Then go on starving yourself to death. What good is that going to do anybody?

PATTI: I'm not starving myself to death.

BO: Sure you are.

PATTI: I am not! *(Silence for a while.)*

PATTI: What does "burn with a blue flame" mean to you, Bo? Tell me so that definition in my head can explode.

BO: One time . . . I don't know if you knew how hard Mary studied . . . she was always working on extra projects and studying those books . . . late at night. I'd kid her sometimes . . . you know . . . just kidding about . . . the fun she was missing and the goofing. But I mean she was having fun. She and Ken . . .

PATTI: Yeah.

BO: But one time . . . this one night . . . when she was up reading her brains out because she was so determined to get to college . . . I said . . . "When you get into college, Mary, you're going to have to read even more." And she said . . . "That's okay by me, Bo, I burn with a blue flame."

PATTI: She said that?

BO: Yeah. Weird, huh.

PATTI: They were just sitting in the car. Talking like we are now. Only about life. And that carbon monoxide was coming in without any warning. "Odorless gas." Odorless gas. It's such a stinking cheat. I know you loved your sister, Bo. I know how bad you feel. I could hardly bear to look at you at the funeral. But I miss Kenny so bad I can't even . . . They were just on a goddamned date. I keep playing it back and I roll their windows down so the air can get in. Pardon me, lovebirds, I say; but I'm just giving you some air. Some clean air so you won't have a death that makes no sense to anybody. Bo, we've gotten so used to crazy violent deaths but not the cheating of carbon monoxide. They didn't even know they were going down and I'll never hear him laugh again. Never. He never knew how much I loved him.

BO: Course he did.

PATTI: I keep playing it back and I roll down the windows. I mean if the windows were just rolled down a crack Bo, they'd be okay wouldn't they, Bo? Even just one window rolled down a crack with clean air coming in. Bo, Christ, he's the only one who ever talked to me and now I'll never see my brother again.

(PATTI is crying uncontrollably now. BO has his arms around her and she cries against him as he comforts her.)

BO: We're all rolling down the windows, Patti.

PATTI: I loved him so much.

BO: I know, I know.

Album

by David Rimmer

The Play

Please refer to synopsis for this play on page 7.

The Scene

Trish's best friend, Peggy, has just returned from summer camp. Trish immediately wants to know about Peggy's sexual adventures and if she is still a virgin. The scene begins with Trish's parents asking her to turn down her blaring music.

> (TRISH, 16, is sprawled on the floor downstage, one hand hold-
> ing up a picture of John Lennon, as she gazes at it, a transistor
> radio next to her, blaring. She's wearing summer clothes, shorts
> and a sleeveless blouse; her body is beginning to fill out, she's
> looking more like a girl, her hair a little longer, more in control,
> her face less hidden. She listens to an offstage voice and reluc-
> tantly responds to it.)
>
> TRISH: Okay! Okay! (She grudgingly turns down the radio, and
> the volume of "Ticket to Ride" goes down. She gets up, muttering
> and grumbling as she walks around the room in frustration.) Ha-
> ven't you gone yet? . . . God . . . (She looks out the window and
> hears the sound of a car starting up and pulling away. She yells.)

I'll listen as loud as I want! (Afraid she said it too loud, she takes a quick look outside, then, relieved, goes to her radio, and turns it back up. She sings along with the second verse of the song, changing the lyrics to show her anger toward her parents: from "She" and "me" to "I" and "you." As she sings, she takes out her mother's picture album and a pen, and a pack of cigarettes with matches and ashtray — all hidden under the bed. She sits on the floor and defiantly lights a cigarette. After a second or two of pleasure, the smoke gets in her eyes, and she reacts in pain. Then she turns her attention to the album, leafing through it, writing in it, turning down the radio a bit.) Writin' in your sacred old picture album again, Mom. "A Thousand Stars," "Surfer Girl." Ecch. Ancient history. *(Smiles.)* "Eight Days A Week," "Help!" "Ticket To Ride." Here's what happens, Mom: I meet John Lennon at a party and he needs help just like a regular person, he's having problems with Cynthia and he's just waiting for the right bird to fly away with and I'm it and we run away together and leave you and your old album behind. And he's my Ticket to Ride. . . . *(She kisses the picture of John on the lips; then gets up.)* Sick. Gotta stop fallin' in love with pictures. *(Looks out the window.)* C'mon, get dark. *(The sound of a car pulling into the driveway scares her. She fans the air for smoke, hides the cigarettes, runs to the window.)* Shit! Back already? Can't you give me any peace —? *(Yelps in delight.)* Peggy! *(Looks closer.)* Barb? And a guy —? *(She runs out the door as the radio plays, and after a second or two, she and* PEGGY, *16 too, rush back into the room.* PEGGY *is wearing summer clothes, looks great in them. She seems the same, maybe a little more cynical and bored; no cracks in her front yet. They're playfully arguing, giggling like crazy, words overlapping, as they run to the window, music slowly fading down and out.)*

PEGGY: I had the worst summer of all time.

TRISH: No, I had the worst summer of all time.

PEGGY: No, I did — *Wait!* What's Barb doin'?

TRISH: Who's that guy, he looks so hoody — Move!

PEGGY: I can't see! God, I can't believe she's gonna do it with him —

TRISH: Do what?

PEGGY: It.

TRISH: *It?* You mean — How do you know? How can you tell?

PEGGY: She told me.

TRISH: Oh.

PEGGY: Wait! He's bending down! Look!

TRISH: Oh my God, he's goin' for it already! *(Sound of car engine gunning.)*

PEGGY: Nah, he's just revvin' it up. What a grub. Rory. *(They both giggle.)* She could've picked a guy with a better name.

TRISH: And one that didn't look like he just got out of state prison. *(Sounds of the car pulling away; they watch it drive out of sight.)*

PEGGY: She said to stay here and wait for her 'til she gets back. Then she'll tell us all about it.

TRISH: God, you go away for a summer and look what happens. You didn't do it too, didya?

PEGGY: Wanna hear somethin' sad? Midnight died —

TRISH: Your cat?

PEGGY: He got hit by a car. Splat. *(PEGGY starts checking out the room.)* Oh my God, you got your own phone now? *(Picks up the receiver, speaks into it.)* Princess. *(Sits on the bed, looks into the album.)* And still gettin' hot over pictures . . .?

TRISH: Shut up! What about Barb?

PEGGY: What about her?

TRISH: The first time you do it, it hurts, doesn't it? And it bleeds?

PEGGY: I guess.

TRISH: *(Wondrous.)* But only for a second. Then every time afterwards it doesn't . . . Hey —

PEGGY: *What?*

TRISH: Do you think — no —

PEGGY: *What?*

TRISH: You think you'd — Think you'd ever do it with one of the Beatles?

PEGGY: *Dugan!* — God! —

TRISH: If you had the chance —

PEGGY: I don't know —

TRISH: Would you? —

PEGGY: Cut it out —

TRISH: *Come on,* would you? —

PEGGY: All right, yeah, I guess so —

TRISH: Which one?

PEGGY: Dugan, gimme a break. Haven't you gotten over the Beatles yet?

TRISH: I'll never get over them —

PEGGY: *(Leafing through album.)* I remember when it was Brian Wilson and the Beach Boys.

TRISH: Bullshit.

PEGGY: You kiss your mother with that mouth?

TRISH: *(Sighs.)* I've never even seen a boy's, you know.

PEGGY: I saw my brother's in the bathtub once. *(They both giggle.)*

TRISH: Really? What'd it look like?

PEGGY: Like a mushroom. With a little eye at the end of it. Then when it gets big, it's like a mushroom on top of a rocket.

TRISH: It gets big? I thought it just, you know, stood up. Like an erection. *(Hesitant pause.)* Do you know, um, do the balls go in with it or do they stay outside?

PEGGY: *(Embarrassed.)* Gross!

TRISH: My mother never told me anything she was supposed to. She said stuff like, "A kiss should end the evening, not begin it." And "Why buy a cow when you can already taste the milk?"

PEGGY: What does that mean?

TRISH: Don't do it before you're married.

PEGGY: Vomitous.

TRISH: I wonder if Barb'll have to get married.

PEGGY: *Will you shut up about Barb?*

TRISH: What's the matter? You did it too, didn't you?

PEGGY: No, I — Never mind.

TRISH: Some friend. You and Barb go off and do it and leave me — *(Stops and stares at* PEGGY.*)*

PEGGY: What're you doin'?

TRISH: Tryin' to see if you look different.

PEGGY: What?

TRISH: You look different after you do it. That's what happens.

PEGGY: How can you look different?

TRISH: I don't know! You turn into a woman and you look different. Don't ask me. *(Beat.)* You look the same to me. Didya feel different after you did it?

PEGGY: *Will you leave me alone?*

TRISH: What's the matter?

PEGGY: No — I — did — not — feel — different.

TRISH: Why not?

PEGGY: *Dugan!*

TRISH: Peggy . . . What —? Aren't you gonna tell me about it?

PEGGY: Why?

TRISH: 'Cause you're my friend, that's why.

PEGGY: Why don't you just wait for Barb to get back. She's your friend too.

TRISH: 'Cause — She's not my friend the way you are. Okay? *'Cause I want you to tell me!* (PEGGY *smiles, drifts off for a second, glances at some of* TRISH's *old toys.*)

PEGGY: Remember that time when we were little kids and we became blood sisters?

TRISH: Yeah, and the knife slipped and I got an infection. I still got the scar.

PEGGY: Lemme see. (TRISH *holds out her hand.* PEGGY *takes it in hers, holds it, then bites it.* TRISH *cries "Ow!", backs away, her hand at her mouth, sucking at the sore.*)

TRISH: You're weird. God, if it changes you this much, I don't know if I wanna do it.

PEGGY: *(Coming over to her.)* I'm sorry! I'm sorry, I just wanted to be blood sisters again. *(She takes* TRISH's *hand and gently kisses it on the sore spot and then walks away. Amazed,* TRISH *just stares at her.)* I met this guy from another town. I didn't even know his name.

TRISH: God . . .

PEGGY: Shh — Don't talk. *(Beat.)* I drove down to the Quarry with him, and we parked the car. (TRISH *sits down, listening, all rapt attention.*) There wasn't anybody else there. There was a full moon, I could see it through the windshield. We got in the back seat . . . 1st Base, 2nd Base, 3rd Base . . . He kept touching me down there. You remember the first time you felt . . . you got wet?

TRISH: Tell me about now.

PEGGY: First time it happened to me was way back with Billy. That was nice. *(Looks at* TRISH, *who's still anxiously waiting.)* Okay, we're in the back seat, and practically all our clothes are off. Then he goes and gets a rubber. Eeuu. And he gets on top of me and starts moanin' and groanin' like he was dyin' or something. Then I feel something touching me down there and I think, "Okay, okay, it's only gonna hurt a second." But it keeps hurting, and it isn't going in. I said, "What's the matter?" And he said, "No, it's okay, it's okay." He wanted me to put my hand on it. It was all slimy. And he keeps trying and trying and it still won't go in. He was sweating on me. I felt so squished. I pushed him off me, and he was just sitting there with this stupid look on his face, and I thought, "This is it?" So I said to him, "There's something wrong with one of us." He didn't say anything.

TRISH: *(Her face fallen.)* That isn't true.

PEGGY: I'm never doin' it again. First and last.

TRISH: *(Can't believe it.)* That happened to *you?*

PEGGY: No, it happened to Shelley Fabares. *(*TRISH *just stares at* PEGGY, *who keeps her face turned away. Pause. The phone rings.* TRISH, *never taking her eyes off* PEGGY, *answers it.)*

TRISH: Hello? . . . Barb? . . . What —? *(listens)* . . . God . . . Yeah, where are ya? . . . Okay, we'll be right there. . . . I promise. . . . Just keep listenin' to your radio, okay? . . . What —? They played "Satisfaction" and now they're playin' "Wooly Bully"? Great. Okay, we're comin'. Bye. *(Hangs up. Stands there stunned.)* She started doin' it with the guy, and he asked if she was a virgin or not. She said yeah, he said forget it, and he kicked her out of the car and left her on the beach.

PEGGY: Figures.

TRISH: How're you supposed to get to *not* be a virgin? *(*TRISH *stands still, not sure what to do.* PEGGY *lies down on the bed and looks at* TRISH's *pictures.* TRISH *puts her sandals on, then turns back to* PEGGY.*)* Come on . . . We better go. . . .

PEGGY: Maybe it's better with pictures. *(*TRISH *yanks* PEGGY *up and they both go out the door, arms around each other.)*

Only Children

by Josh Cagan

The Play

Cara and Kay are estranged sisters in their twenties. When they were young girls, they both idolized their father, but now Cara has deliberately and mysteriously cut him out of her life. Cara has moved out of the state, leaving behind no forwarding address. Kay, having obtained her new address, arrives to bring her home because their father has suffered a heart attack and is dying.

The Scene

Cara is in bed reading a love letter written to her father by his girlfriend. Her little sister, Kay, has just barged into her room. Cara tries to keep the letter from her sister but Kay insists on reading it. Cara, shattered by her father's betrayal, wants to tell their mother. Kay, loyal to their father and afraid of divorce, insists that Cara throw the letter away.

> *(Area Two. The house is notably cleaner. KAY is relaxing on the couch, reading one of CARA's notebooks.)*

KAY: "Cara Observes . . ." How pretentious. Hm. *(She scans through.)* "Cara observes on her family, or, what's left of it," Blah, blah, blah . . . "Plenty of families doggedly stick together, no matter how bad they might be for each other," Sob, sob, sob . . . "Joyless

Christmas dinners . . . Dry, scratchy Thanksgiving turkeys,"
Angst, angst, angst . . . "Put it all together, and you have a genetic
train wreck . . . Four people who have no business together . . . And that's where I come in. Or, rather, that's where I
went out. I didn't ask to be born into this family, so I quit." Hip,
hip, hooray. Man, Shaun. I don't see how you can live with her.
Whiny, artsy, no-good . . . *(She flips through the notebook, and
finds an old letter on pink stationery.)* Oh. Shit.
*(Lights up on Area One. CARA at 15 is seated on the bed, hold-
ing the same pink envelope. KAY and CARA at 15 pull out the
letter at the same time. They begin to read.)*

KAY AND CARA AT 15: "Dear Thomas . . ."
 (Lights fade on Area Two.)

CARA AT 15: "Dear Thomas. I love you so much, and I miss
 you . . . Last night was amazing . . . Sometimes, when you and I
 are just lying there, I close my eyes and pretend you're all mine. I
 know you can't leave your family, and I don't want you
 to . . . Right now. But I'll wait until you realize how happy you
 are with me. And I think you already do . . . I know it's just a matter of time before we don't have to sneak around, and I can hardly
 wait. Until then, I don't mind leasing you, because I know I'll
 have the option to buy someday. Looking forward to next weekend . . . Love Tina."
 *(KAY comes barging in, SHAUN in tow, and clicks off the light.
 CARA shoves the letter under a pillow.)*

KAY AT 11: *(Holding flashlight under face.)* BOO!

CARA AT 15: I swear to GOD, Kay. If you come in here without
 knocking one more time —

KAY AT 11: *(Turning the lights on.)* Were you doing something bad?

CARA AT 15: No, I wasn't doing anything bad. Shouldn't you be
 asleep?

KAY AT 11: Shouldn't you?

CARA AT 15: I'm older, I get to stay up later.

KAY AT 11: How was going to dad's work?

CARA AT 15: Fine, I guess.

KAY AT 11: Did you see any rock stars?

CARA AT 15: Kay, he works at an A.M. sports station.

KAY AT 11: Oh. *(Pause.)* Did you see any sports stars?

CARA AT 15: Yeah. Babe Ruth was there. He gave us all candy bars.
 Look, can you go away? I'm . . . I'm trying to get some sleep.

KAY AT 11: With your lights on?

CARA AT 15: I'm . . . About to be trying to get some sleep. And if mom catches you up, she's gonna . . .

KAY AT 11: She's not gonna do anything, dad'll get me out of it.

CARA AT 15: Well, dad had to go . . . *(Sighs.)* Back to the station. Which means that anything that mom doles out'll be effective until tomorrow night. Or whenever he feels like coming back.

KAY AT 11: He's there a lot.

CARA AT 15: Yep.

KAY AT 11: Was it really cool there? Like he says? A lot of people running around bumping into each other? Like popcorn when it's popping?

CARA AT 15: Why don't you ask him?

KAY AT 11: 'Cause he's not here and you are!

CARA AT 15: Well, I don't feel like talking about it. Okay? So bug off!

KAY AT 11: Sor-RY.

CARA AT 15: Look, just get out of here. Go to sleep.

(KAY AT 11 *walks toward the door, and then walks back and plops herself next to* CARA.)

KAY AT 11: Can I sleep here tonight?

CARA AT 15: Oh, you gotta be kidding me.

KAY AT 11: I'll just camp on the floor. I won't make any noise. Swear to god.

CARA AT 15: You've got a perfectly good room.

KAY AT 11: It's cold in there.

CARA AT 15: Have mom turn the heat up.

KAY AT 11: Come on, Cara. Please?

CARA AT 15: NO! Get the outta my room!

(KAY AT 11 *begins to sniffle.*)

CARA AT 15: Oh, lord. I'm sorry. Don't start.

KAY AT 11: *(Quietly, sing-songy.)* Mommmmy . . .

CARA AT 15: Fine, fine. Sleep in here. Knock yourself out. Shh . . . Shhh.

KAY AT 11: *(Pause.)* Aw-sum. Gimmie a blanket.

CARA AT 15: Go get one of yours.

KAY AT 11: Mom might see that I'm up!

CARA AT 15: You were just about to whine for her.

KAY AT 11: Yeah, but that woulda gotten you in trouble.

CARA AT 15: Of course.

(CARA *walks over to her closet to get a blanket.*
KAY *grabs* CARA's *pillow.*)

KAY AT 11: I need a pillow too.

CARA AT 15: Kay!

(KAY AT 11 *grabs the letter.*)

KAY AT 11: What's this?

CARA AT 15: Nothing. *(She grabs the letter.)*

KAY AT 11: Is it a letter to you?

CARA AT 15: Yeah, sure.

KAY AT 11: No it's not! It said, "Dear Thomas." That's dad's name. You took one of dad's letters! Was this in his office?

CARA AT 15: BEDTIME!

(CARA *turns off the lights.* KAY *turns on her flashlight, and uses it to grill* CARA.)

CARA AT 15: Look —

KAY AT 11: You stole stuff from dad's office!

CARA AT 15: We're not gonna talk —

KAY AT 11: You better tell me what it is, or I'm gonna tell mom and dad that you stole.

CARA AT 15: Cool. I'd almost like to see what they said.

KAY AT 11: Tell me what it is!

CARA AT 15: No.

KAY AT 11: Tell me.

CARA AT 15: No.

KAY AT 11: *(Points flashlight at* CARA's *replacements poster.)* Getting excited about the big concert?

CARA AT 15: Shut up . . .

KAY AT 11: Bet it's gonna be fine . . .

CARA AT 15: Kay . . .

KAY AT 11: Sure would suck if you couldn't go . . .

CARA AT 15: SHUT UP! Read the stupid letter. *(She tosses it to her, and turns the lights on.)*

KAY AT 11: *(Reading.)* "Dear Thomas . . . I love you so much . . . " Ew. "I miss you . . . " Cara, you tard. This is just a love letter from mom. Like that's such a big deal.

CARA AT 15: Guess you don't have to read the rest of it then.

KAY AT 11: I guess I do.

KAY AT 11: *(Reading.)* "Love, Tina." Who's Tina?

CARA AT 15: Not mom. *(Pause.)*

KAY AT 11: Oh. *(Pause. Tossing the letter at* CARA.) Well, goodnight.

(KAY AT 11 *settles down on a beanbag.*)

CARA AT 15: Goodnight?

KAY AT 11: See you tomorrow.

CARA AT 15: Kay. Do you get what's going on?

KAY AT 11: Could you turn out the lights?

CARA AT 15: Kay. Dad's fooling around. That's why he's late all the time. That's why he's away on trips. He's with someone who's not mom!

KAY AT 11: It's a practical joke or something. I'm trying to sleep.

CARA AT 15: *(Pause.)* I'm gonna show it to mom.

KAY AT 11: *(Bolting up.)* You do that, and I'm never gonna speak to you again.

CARA AT 15: Well, if it's just a joke . . .

KAY AT 11: Cara, you should throw that stupid thing away. Or put it back where you found it. It's . . . Stupid. And mom shouldn't see it.

CARA AT 15: So what? Pretend like I never found it?

KAY AT 11: Yes. Now . . . Let's go to sleep. Please.

CARA AT 15: Jesus Christ, Kay. That's exactly what you'd like us to do. Just sleep . . . Just ignore . . . Whatever. Dad's the greatest guy in the world, he can do no wrong . . . He's perfect. Except that he's almost never home. And when he is home, him and mom don't talk. And he's always giving us presents and stuff, like that'll shut us up.

KAY AT 11: He's taking me horseback riding this weekend.

CARA AT 15: That's exactly what I mean. And that makes this okay? *(Holds up envelope.)* Sleep if you want. I'm awake. I'm showing it to mom.

KAY AT 11: *(Standing, and speaking matter of factly.)* Cara, if you tell mom about this . . . I will tell her about every bad thing you've ever done. I will start with your concert, and work my way backwards. I will tell her about when that boy snuck up here last year. I will tell her about the bad progress reports I found in your closet. I will tell her that when we were little, you made me eat dirt.

CARA AT 15: So what? Mom and dad aren't gonna care! They'll be too busy . . .

KAY AT 11: Getting divorced!

CARA AT 15: Maybe.

KAY AT 11: I don't want mom and dad to stop being married. I don't want to move to a smaller house and share a room with mom like my friend Patti did. I don't want to go to a different school.

CARA AT 15: Why is this suddenly all about you?

KAY AT 11: Do you want that stuff to happen?

(Pause.)
KAY AT 11: Do you, Cara?
CARA AT 15: I . . . Well, no. But —
KAY AT 11: So promise me.
    (Pause.)
KAY AT 11: 5, 4, 3, 2 . . . *(Pause.)* 2 . . .
CARA AT 15: I promise. Okay. I promise.
KAY AT 11: *(Gives her a big hug.)* Goodnight.
    (KAY AT 11 lies down and goes to sleep.)
CARA AT 15: Yeah. Pleasant dreams.
    (Lights up on Area Two. CARA AT 15 and KAY close the letters in their respective notebooks.)
KAY: You promised. *(Lights fade on Area One. KAY puts the notebook down on the coffee table.)* Goddamnit, Shaun, she promised. *(Lights fade on Area Two.)*

Nobody Dies

by David Rimmer

The Play

Nobody Dies starts early in the morning on the day after college graduation for four 22-year-old kids crashing in the parentless home of a slightly older guy and his 14-year-old brother, which is not far from the campus in their little college town. They think the house is going to be a pleasant summer way station for them between the Ivory Tower of college and the Big World outside, but soon find harsh reality crashing in the door. A crucial event early in the day sets in motion primal family, sexual, and romantic conflicts as well as issues of betrayal, abandonment, and withdrawal of love and threatens to destroy the alternative family unit these people have created. The play, which veers from wild physical comedy to intense drama, takes place in one day in 1970, from dawn to midnight.

The Scene

Barb and Rita, college seniors and best friends, are hanging out at home watching a movie. The guys have gone out drinking. Donna, seventeen, who spent the night with their twenty-six-year-old roommate Johnny, is drawn to this "family" and has come back for the stuffed animal that Johnny won for her at the carnival. Rita, who is more experienced sexually than Barb, uses Donna as a middleman to get Barb to open up about her sexual issues.

MIDNIGHT
"The Way Young Lovers Do," Van Morrison, plays.
Lights up: faint, shifting, changing colors — no lamps on in the house, just the color TV.
BARB and RITA lie on a blanket DR, watching an old movie on TV without the sound on, eating cookies, drinking soda. BARB's wearing a tank top that was under the loose shirt she had on before; her hair's down — she looks sexier. MUSIC OUT.

RITA: Catch this entrance here —
BARB: Oh my God — that dress!
RITA: What's it made of — fiberglass?
BARB: I love this color —
RITA: Yeah, look at her hair — it's blue —
BARB: *(Calls to UL door.)* Danny? . . . *Danny!* You want to watch TV?
DANNY: *(Off.)* No!
BARB: Want something to eat?
DANNY: *(Off.)* Not hungry!
    (BARB sighs; the girls stare at the TV.)
RITA: It's so much better without the sound.
BARB: *(Impatient glance at front door.)* What're we doing here?
RITA: I'm trying to watch a movie.
BARB: Where are those guys?
    (Knock on the front door. BARB and RITA look at each other, shrug.)
BARB: Come in.
    (DONNA enters.)
BARB/RITA: Donna.
DONNA: Hi.
BARB/RITA: Hi.
DONNA: I snuck out. My parents were watching this stupid movie on TV — Oh, that's it.
BARB/RITA: Yeah — / Pretty stupid —
DONNA: I just came back to get something — *(Sees the stuffed dog on the couch.)* What's it doing out here?
BARB/RITA: Um — / Uh — well —
DONNA: *(Sees how messed up it is.)* What happened?
RITA: There was a fight.
BARB: Sorry.
DONNA: Maybe I should go.

(She starts to — they stop her.)

BARB/RITA: No, don't go — / Come on, it's okay —

DONNA: *(Tentatively moves to the blanket.)* Okay.

BARB/RITA: Soda? / Cookies? Oreos! . . .

DONNA: No thank you.

    (Uncomfortable beat.)

BARB: Make yourself at   DONNA: Is Johnny here? —
home —   Oh — excuse me —

BARB: Go ahead —   DONNA: Go ahead —

BARB: You go ahead.

DONNA: No, you —

BARB: No, it's okay —

RITA: Barb? Shut up. Donna? Talk.

DONNA: I was just asking if Johnny was here, I — *(She heads to the bedroom.)*

RITA: So Donna, what's Johnny like in there?

BARB: Rita!

RITA: Well! He must be pretty good if both Donna and Betsy —

    (DONNA comes back, after a quick glance inside.)

DONNA: Johnny and Betsy had something really special, didn't they?

RITA: No, she was just bored with college boys. C'mon, sit down. Where'd you meet him?

DONNA: *(Sits.)* At the Carnival, last night. But I knew who he was. I kinda went up to him. He won me the dog — all of a sudden I'm on the back of his bike, headin' downtown, goin' so fast I — here I am.

BARB: You really like him, huh? *(DONNA shrugs.)* Was he your first?

DONNA: He was the first I used birth control with.

    (BARB chokes on some soda.)

    What about you and Kid?

BARB: What about us? — I mean — there's no us —

DONNA: Isn't he your . . . ?

BARB: We're friends. We'll stay friends, I guess, but we probably won't see each other that much — After college everybody goes their own way, you know —

RITA: Donna, Barb's really full of shit.

BARB: What?

RITA: I'm sure she won't mind me telling you that she's never had an easy time with sex —

BARB: *What?!*

RITA: Don't you remember? Your first time with that kinda hoodlum guy?

(Confidentially to DONNA.*)*

She didn't even know him or anything, it was just cause all the other girls were doing it, you know. She was 17.

DONNA: I'm 17.

RITA: Then you'll understand. Well, y'know, it wasn't that much fun for her and that kept her away from it for a while. Until she came here.

BARB: Rita, do you mind?

RITA: What's wrong?

BARB: You know what's wrong.

RITA: Yeah, I do, but Donna doesn't. — Anyway, when she gets here, she meets the guy she knows'll change everything for her —

DONNA: Kid?

RITA: Barb?

BARB: *What.*

RITA: Donna asked you a question.

BARB: *Rita.*

RITA: Oh that is so rude! Donna wants to know — right?

DONNA: Right, I do.

RITA: *(Looks at* BARB, *who clams up;* RITA *sighs with exasperation.)* Okay, so what happened was that right after she met him and right before she went out with him, she had this kind of strange experience — Nothing worth talking about, but when it came to having sex with him, things just got — *(Prodding* BARB.*)* Things just got . . . ?

BARB: What do you want from me?

RITA: C'mon, you got this far!

BARB: *You* got this far!

RITA: *(Quiet command.)* Tell her.

BARB: Okay, things got weird, I got scared and I couldn't go through with it, all right?

RITA: Bad timing —

BARB: And he got all freaked out like it was his fault or something —

RITA: Wasn't anybody's fault really —

BARB: — Thanks Rita. — But that's what he thought.

RITA: Yeah, it kind of screwed things up with him for a while, but they always stayed friends. And he's had a few since, and she's had a few . . . and she kinda got back to normal — for her — but, y'know, she always finds a way to break up with them before things get too heavy. And meanwhile, right across campus, guess who's doing the exact same thing?

DONNA: Kid?

RITA: You'd think they'd figure it out by now. They're book-smart, y'know, but they're people-stupid. What would you do?

DONNA: *(To BARB.)* You love him, don't you?

BARB: I —

DONNA: Why don't you tell him?

RITA: Why didn't *you* think of that?

BARB: *(Fist up.)* You're gonna get it.

RITA: *You* are.

    (SOUND of a car screeching into the driveway — BARB *and* RITA *look out the window.)*

BARB: It's them —

Blue Denim

by James Leo Herlihy and William Noble

The Play

Set in Detroit, *Blue Denim* revolves around fifteen-year-old Arthur, the son of a retired army officer, who discovers that he is about to become a father. Arthur feels helpless and has never been close enough to his parents to go to them for advice. When he does, at his friend Ernie's urging, he cannot make himself understood. The play brings home the problems of communication between the older and younger generations.

The Scene

Arthur and Janet have decided that an abortion is the only answer to their problem. Arthur, remembering that Ernie mentioned that he knew of that kind of a "doctor," has invited Ernie to his home to talk.

> (ARTHUR *picks up the sheets, wraps them around his neck thoughtlessly, then drapes them over his head.*)

ERNIE: Well, you going to turn it off or aren't you?
ARTHUR: *(From under the sheets.)* Shut up. (ARTHUR *sits on the day bed, listlessly places his hands over his sheet-covered face.*)

ERNIE: I'm on your side, y'know. But if you *don't* turn the tank off the whole house'll blow up and they'll blame it all on you. I can just see the fire engines screaming up Seven Mile Road — and your old man standing out front in his nightshirt with a row o' World War ribbons across his chest.

ARTHUR: My old man wears pajamas.

ERNIE: Pajamas, then. And Lillian and your ma with their hair up in curlers bawling hell out of you 'cause you wouldn't turn off the hot-water tank.

(ARTHUR *rips the sheets from his face and takes them to the far corner of the basement, where he deposits them in a laundry basket. Then he opens the door under the stairway and turns off the tank.*)

ARTHUR: You know something, Ernie? You're getting on my nerves lately. You're always talking. You don't know how to just plain shut up. Sorry, but that's one o' your faults. Maybe you don't even realize it even.

ERNIE: I don't get it. Invite me over to talk about something serious — and when I get here all I get is a big lecture about how nervous I make you. *(Gathering cards together.)* Oh, well, this isn't coming out right, anyhow.

ARTHUR: Sit down.

ERNIE: Nah, I think I'll go home and give your nerves a rest.

ARTHUR: *(Pushing him back into the chair.)* Sit down, I said. I do want to talk to you. Only . . .

ERNIE: Yeah?

ARTHUR: I just hadn't got around to it yet — You know what you said once about a doctor that does operations on girls?

ERNIE: On girls?

ARTHUR: Don't act square!

ERNIE: I'm not acting square. What doctor?

ARTHUR: You said, Clifford Truckston came to you when his girl was in trouble.

ERNIE: Art, so help me —

ARTHUR: *(Standing over him.)* You know what I'm talking about. Don't act square, I said!

ERNIE: Okay, I remember.

ARTHUR: Well, I met a guy the other day wants to get hold of that doctor.

ERNIE: *What* guy?

ARTHUR: I can't say; I swore I wouldn't tell a soul.

ERNIE: Well, you better not tell *me*, then.

ARTHUR: He's a real nice guy. He really is. A friend of the family, you know, kind of like a cousin, only he's *not* my cousin.

ERNIE: Where's he live?

ARTHUR: Hazel Park.

ERNIE: How come you never mentioned him before?

ARTHUR: I said, he's a friend of the family. *(When* ERNIE *does not answer.)* I promised him and he's counting on me, Ernie. I told him all about you, and how you know everything.

ERNIE: *(A little sickly.)* Yeah?

ARTHUR: Yeah. I told him what a swell guy you are and — he said he'd like to meet you sometime.

ERNIE: Look, Art, I'd like to help this bird, but you don't want to get mixed up in it. I mean, hell, you could get thrown in jail so fast it'd make your teeth chatter. Abortion's a crime. It's murder.

ARTHUR: *(Intensely.)* The hell it is! *(*ARTHUR *grips* ERNIE*'s wrist tightly.)* Always yakkin'! Always running off at the mouth!

ERNIE: Hey, leggo, Art.

ARTHUR: *(Not letting go.)* Tell me!

ERNIE: Tell you what?

ARTHUR: The doctor!

ERNIE: *(Trying to rise.)* You're awful hard to get along with lately, Art. Pretty soon you won't have any friends left if you keep on *(*ARTHUR *pushes the card table out of the way and grips* ERNIE*'s head in the crook of one arm; with the other he restrains* ERNIE*'s resistance.)*

ARTHUR: Who is he? Where's he live?

ERNIE: You're chokin' me!

ARTHUR: *(Applying greater pressure.)* You gonna tell?

ERNIE: Leggo, you stupid sonofabitch!

*(*ARTHUR *forces* ERNIE *to the floor, straddles him with one knee on his chest, his hands clenched around his throat.)*

ARTHUR: *(Hysterical.)* You're not stupid, are you, Ernie! Know all the answers! Know everything! Just ask Ernie! *(Then, in a hoarse whisper, inclining his head toward* ERNIE *until their faces almost touch.)* That baby's getting bigger and bigger every minute!

ERNIE: Art, if you kill me they'll put you in jail!

ARTHUR: Tell me!

ERNIE: I can't! I was lying!

> (ARTHUR *releases his grip on* ERNIE. *He slumps into a chair and stares at the floor.*)

ARTHUR: *(Dully)* You were lying? Why?

ERNIE: I dunno, Art. I just thought of saying it — and out it came.

ARTHUR: Yeah.

ERNIE: Don't be mad, Art. *(A small nervous laugh.)* Maybe I got a big-shot complex or something. 'Cause I'm little — and kinda skinny — and . . .

ARTHUR: *(Quietly.)* Ernie, what am I gonna do?

ARNIE: *(Rising to a sitting position.)* What're . . . *you* gonna do? *(Staring reverently at* ARTHUR.*)* I'll find out for you, Art. *(Throwing his right arm into the air.)* I swear to God may my father be struck dead! Who's the g-girl? Never mind, you don't have to tell me. *(A pause.)* That was all true about Truckston. Only he didn't come to me. I just heard about it.

ARTHUR: *(Quietly pleading.)* Where, Ernie? Where'd you hear about it?

ERNIE: At the drugstore. You know that kid with the funny arm? Well, he knows, 'cause the doctor is his uncle or something.

ARTHUR: You sure?

ERNIE: I'm not sure it's his uncle. But I can find out because that kid knows all about it.

ARTHUR: How come you're holding your neck?

ERNIE: No reason.

ARTHUR: I'm sorry, Ernie. I don't know my own strength sometimes.

ERNIE: Good crap, forget it. You got *real* problems. Say I find out about the doctor, where you going to get the money?

ARTHUR: Don't worry, I'll get it. I'll get it if I have to steal it!

ERNIE: That much?

ARTHUR: How much's it cost?

ERNIE: I think a hundred and twenty-five.

ARTHUR: *(Breathing it.)* Brother!

ERNIE: You got any dough at all?

ARTHUR: I got a war bond. The ten years was up on my birthday.

ERNIE: How much?

ARTHUR: Only twenty-five. *You* got any dough?

ERNIE: Not a cent.

ARTHUR: How much could I get for my air rifle? And my bike — I mean if I fixed the tires?

ERNIE: A couple of bucks, maybe. That's just junk. *(Carefully.)* Maybe Janet's got some.

ARTHUR: *(Vehemently.)* Who said anything about *Janet?*

(ERNIE *moves quickly away, holding his neck protectively.)*

ERNIE: Hey, not again!

ARTHUR: Don't tell anybody, Ernie. *(Raising his right hand.)* Swear!

ERNIE: Hell, no, I won't swear. What you got a buddy for if you can't trust him?

ARTHUR: It's just — well, you're always talkin'. It could slip out.

ERNIE: Relax!

ARTHUR: Anyway, Janet's only got eight dollars.

ERNIE: How far along is she?

ARTHUR: I don't know exactly. What's eight and twenty-five? Thirty-three dollars. How much's that leave?

ERNIE: Ninety-two. *If* the price is still a hundred an' a quarter.

ARTHUR: It wouldn't go up, would it? *(There is a pause.)*

ERNIE: Art.

ARTHUR: Yeah?

ERNIE: I suppose you and Janet talked plenty about this?

ARTHUR: O' course we did. Ever since — we found out.

ERNIE: How's she feel about it?

ARTHUR: Just like me. Trapped.

ERNIE: I mean about the operation.

ARTHUR: Janet says she'll do whatever I want.

ERNIE: Sounds like she really loves you.

ARTHUR: Yeah. She does.

ERNIE: But you don't really love her, is that it?

ARTHUR: Sure I do.

ERNIE: Then why don't you get married? If you —

ARTHUR: *(Interrupting angrily.)* We're too young! Listen Ernie. You're the one's always talking about being realistic. Where'd we live? And what *on?*

ERNIE: Maybe you could move in with her dad.

ARTHUR: Nah! He's — he cries.

ERNIE: Maybe here then, with your folks.

ARTHUR: *(Groaning.)* Aw, Ernie! . . . Sometimes you talk like you didn't even know the facts of life.

ERNIE: You talk like your folks didn't.

ARTHUR: *(Seriously.)* Maybe they don't.

ERNIE: You got born, didn't you?

ARTHUR: *(Doubtfully.)* Yeah, but . . . Ernie, answer me something serious. Can you picture my mom and dad in bed together?

ERNIE: *(After careful consideration, shakes his head.)* Hunhunh.

ARTHUR: Neither can I.

ERNIE: Look, Art, I can stand around and be your stooge. Or I can be your friend and tell you what I really think.

ARTHUR: You are my friend!

ERNIE: Yeah, but will you keep your goddam hands off my throat?

ARTHUR: I said I was sorry! I just got excited, is all. Tell me what you think.

ERNIE: If it was me, I'd give up this abortion idea. No kidding, Art.

ARTHUR: How can we? I can't just go upstairs and — *tell* 'em! My mom'd start to shake. When she gets upset, she starts to breathe funny. And my old man just goes up in smoke! A thing like this could *kill* 'em even!

ERNIE: Look, I'm not trying to scare hell out of you or anything, but . . . Well — like I said before — it's murder.

ARTHUR: Don't keep saying that! We didn't mean it to be a baby. It was just her and me, Ernie, we didn't think! . . . Besides, it hasn't even got a heart or a name yet. It's just — trouble. Not a person.

ERNIE: It's *alive,* isn't it? Listen, Art, these operations are dangerous. I mean, the doctors that do it aren't so hot sometimes. That's why they got kicked out of the profession, 'cause they weren't very ethical to start with.

(ARTHUR moves away. ERNIE follows.)

ARTHUR: I don't want to talk about it! It'll turn out all right, it's got to!

ERNIE: Yeah? Say he uses a dirty knife or something and Janet got blood poisoning?

ARTHUR: Shut up!

ERNIE: Or he slipped up some way and killed her, even?

ARTHUR: *(Hysterically.)* Will you shut up!

(ARTHUR throws himself face-down on the bed, grabs the pillow and tries to shut out ERNIE's voice.)

ERNIE: They'd blame it on you, Art; and then what'd you do? Tell 'em you did it 'cause you were scared of your old man? Scared your mother might faint or something? *(ARTHUR groans into the pillow.)* I think you'd better face it, Art. Maybe start off by telling 'em you're going to get married, no matter what they say. Then lead into the baby part — casually.

ARTHUR: *(After a moment, raising himself on his elbows.)* What'll I do, Ernie? Just go up right now?

ERNIE: Sure.

ARTHUR: And just — just *tell* 'em!

ERNIE: Why not? You didn't kill anybody!

ARTHUR: I'm not even gonna stop to think about it!

ERNIE: Art! You're doin' the right thing. You won't be sorry.

> *(ARTHUR quietly ascends the stairs and exits into the kitchen. ERNIE climbs the steps into the yard and exits. ARTHUR appears in the hallway.)*

The Private Ear

by Peter Shaffer

The Play

The shy and awkward Tchaik (Tchaik is the nickname given to him by his friend Ted because he likes classical music, particularly Tchaikovsky) has invited a girl that he met at a concert to his flat for dinner. In the interim, he has built up the image of the girl and romanticized her as another Venus. In order not to appear gauche, Tchaik has asked his man-about-town friend, Ted, to coach him. When the girl arrives, Tchaik has a rude awakening.

The Scene

Tchaik is getting ready for his date. Ted has been shopping for the dinner and some last-minute supplies for a romantic evening.

> *The curtain rises on* TCHAIK's *flat. Music is playing: Mozart on the gramophone. The door bursts open;* TCHAIK *rushes in, in bathrobe and slippers, toweling his head. Throughout the scene he displays agitation and indecision in his preparations. There is an iron plugged into the electric light. He throws the towel on the bed, takes trousers from wardrobe, places them on the table and begins to press them. No result. He tests the iron, realizes it is not hot, looks up at the hanging lamp which is off, puts the iron down on the trousers, runs to left of kitchen door and turns on the wall*

switch. He crosses to the armchair and picks up a paper bag in which there is a deodorant stick, throws bag in wastebasket upstage center and crosses to the dresser, dropping his robe around his waist. He opens the stick and applies it to his armpit — he sniffs it. Satisfied, he applies it to the other. He puts the top on the stick, looks around and sees the iron on his pants. Alarmed, he runs to the table, picks the iron up and gingerly feels it. It is still not warm. He sits in chair above table and looks at it. A transistor is heard through the Mozart and TED enters from left carrying a shopping bag and a small transistor radio, which is playing loudly. He pauses inside the door and looks at TCHAIK. He crosses to the red armchair, drops his bag in it, then crosses to the gramophone and takes the arm off it and switches off the gramophone.

TED: *(As he rushes to the gramophone.)* Christ! D'you know what time it is?

TCHAIK: *(Seated behind table.)* What?

TED: *(Switching off transistor.)* Seven-twenty-two. What the hell have you been up to while I've been doing your shopping? Dreaming, I suppose, as usual.

TCHAIK: I haven't.

TED: You're marvelous! The most important night of your life, and you can't even get yourself dressed. All you can do is listen to bloody music. *(He gets a small vase from dresser.)*

TCHAIK: I wasn't listening. It was just on.

TED: *(Crossing to right of table.)* I bet. And what are you doing now?

TCHAIK: Pressing my trousers. But it won't get hot.

TED: If she's on time you've got eight minutes. *(Crosses to armchair and takes flowers from bag.)* I bought you some flowers. *(Throws transistor on bed.)*

TCHAIK: *(Trying to press pants.)* They're nice. Did I give you enough money?

TED: *(Takes vase and flowers into kitchen and fills vase with water.)* Oh, they're on me. They'll provide that chic touch you're just a tiny bit in need of. *Off:* Did you have a bath?

TCHAIK: Yes.

TED: Did you use that stick I gave you? *(He reenters from kitchen.)*

TCHAIK: Yes.

TED: It's a hot evening. There's no point in taking any chances. *(Puts vase on table.)* Did you take that chlorophyll tablet? *(Sniffing his breath.)*

TCHAIK: Oh, for heaven's sake!

TED: Did you?

TCHAIK: Yes.

TED: I'll do that. *(Takes iron and presses pants.)* You get your shirt on. (TCHAIK *gets his shirt, which is hanging in the upstage window, puts it on and crosses to dresser.)* What are you wearing over that?

TCHAIK: I thought my blazer.

TED: It's a bit schooly, but she'll probably like that. Makes you look boyish. You'll bring out the protective in her. What tie?

TCHAIK: *(Taking blue and white striped tie from dresser.)* I thought this one.

TED: Oh yes, gorgeous. What is it? The Sheffield Young Men's Prayer Club?

TCHAIK: *(Holding it out.)* Don't be daft. What's wrong with it?

TED: *(Takes tie.)* You really don't know, do you? Look: that sort of striped tie, well, it marks you, see? "I'm a twelve-pound-a-week office worker," it says. "Every day I say, Come on five-thirty, and every week I say, Come on Friday night. That's me and I'm contented with my lot." That's what that tie says to me.

TCHAIK: *(He has his shirt on — retrieves tie.)* Well, you've got very good hearing, that's what I say.

TED: Where's that green shantung one I gave you last Christmas?

TCHAIK: I lost it.

TED: Typical.

TCHAIK: *(Putting on tie.)* It isn't. I never lose anything.

TED: I think your subconscious would make you lose anything that was chic.

TCHAIK: That's idiotic. And so's that word.

TED: What? Chic?

TCHAIK: Yes. What's it supposed to mean?

TED: It's French for with it.

TCHAIK: "With it"?

TED: Yes, with it. Which is what you're not, and high time you were. You can't stay in the Provinces all your life, you know. I can't do a thing with this material. You'd better put them on. *(Throws pants to* TCHAIK.*)* Six minutes. *(*TCHAIK *crosses upstage to right of bed and puts on trousers.* TED *stands on chair and unplugs iron.)* You're not going to let me down tonight, are you?

TCHAIK: What do you mean?

TED: *(Crossing to the kitchen, wrapping the cord around the iron as he goes.)* You know what you're going to do this evening? I mean, you know what I'm expecting you to do, don't you? *(Pauses in the door, turns off wall switch, puts iron in kitchen.* TCHAIK *puts robe on bed.* TED *appears in kitchen door.)* Eh?

TCHAIK: *(Sits foot of bed.)* Look, Ted, it's not that way at all.

TED: No?

TCHAIK: No, not at all.

TED: *(Takes shopping bag into kitchen.)* Well then, I'm wasting my time here, aren't I? With all due respect, mate, there are rival attractions to playing chef to you, you know. Do you know where I could be tonight? This very night? Takes out his wallet and selects a photo.

TCHAIK: Where?

TED: With her! Look. *(Shows* TCHAIK *photo.)*

TCHAIK: Goodness.

TED: How about them for a pair of bubbles? And that hair — you can't keep your hands off it. It's what they call raven.

TCHAIK: Raven?

TED: Raven black. It's got tints of blue in it. *(He crosses center.)*

TCHAIK: Where did you meet this one? *(Puts on socks.)*

TED: *(Left of table.)* In the Whisky A Go-Go, last night, twisting herself giddy with some little nit. I sort of detached her. She only wanted a date for tonight, didn't she? But I said, "Sorry, doll, no can do. I'm engaged for one night only, at great expense, as chef to my mate Tchaik, who is entertaining a bird of his own. *Très special occasion.*" *(The second sock has a large hole in it, through which* TCHAIK*'s toes appear.)* Come on! *(*TED *has seen this and motions* TCHAIK *to the dresser for a fresh pair.* TCHAIK *crosses to dresser, gets another pair from the top drawer, and returns to the bed.* TED *folds the blanket from the table and throws it in the wardrobe.)* So be grateful. Greater love hath no man, than to pass up a bird like this for his mate. *(*TED *picks up photo from bed and leans it against vase on table.)* Look at the way she holds herself. That's what they used to call carriage. You don't see too much of that nowadays. Most of the girls I meet think they've got it, ignorant little nits. That is the genuine article, that is. Carriage. Miss Carriage.

TCHAIK: *(Who now has socks and one shoe on — going into the kitchen.)* What's her name?

TED: You won't believe me if I tell you. Lavinia.

TCHAIK: Lavinia?

TED: *(Sits armchair.)* Honest. How's that for a sniff of class? The rest of it isn't so good. Botty. Lavinia Botty.

TCHAIK: *(Reentering with tray on which are three knives, forks, spoons, napkins, place mats, tumblers, and a pitcher of water and a salt cellar.)* She's beautiful.

TED: Do you think so?

TCHAIK: *(Puts tray on chair above table.)* Yes.

TED: She's going to go off fairly quickish. In three years she'll be all lumpy, like old porridge.

TCHAIK: *(Crosses to dresser, gets tablecloth.)* I don't know how you do it. I don't, honest.

TED: *(Raising the upstage leaf of table.)* Just don't promise them anything, that's all. Make no promises, they can't hang anything on you, can they? *(As* TCHAIK *lays the cloth,* TED *picks up vase and photo, then replaces them on the cloth.)*

TCHAIK: I wouldn't know.

TED: Well you're going to, after tonight.

TCHAIK: *(Protesting.)* Ted!

TED: Here. I heard a good one the other day. The National Gallery just paid ten thousand pounds for a picture of a woman with five breasts. D'you know what it's called?

TCHAIK: What?

TED: "Sanctity."

TCHAIK: *(Not understanding.)* Sanctity.

TED: Un, deux, trois, quatre, cinq . . . *(*TCHAIK *crosses to kitchen door, puzzled. Turns to give a grin of comprehension and exits with tray.)* What do you call this, laying a table?

TCHAIK: *(Reenters and picks up the other shoe.)* What's wrong with it?

TED: We're all left-handed, are we?

TCHAIK: Oh, lord. *(He hurries to re-lay the table. In his haste he upsets the vase.)*

TED: Well, get a cloth. *(TCHAIK scurries onto the balcony to get it.)* You've wet my Lavinia. We'll have to dry you out, love. *(He crosses and puts her in the mirror. TCHAIK crosses down and begins to mop the table.)* You've got the pit-a-pats. Now look Tchaik, if you get in a state, the evening will be a fiasco. So sit there and calm down.

TCHAIK: *(Sits in the armchair and puts on his other shoe.)* I am calm.

TED: *(Crosses into kitchen.)* After all, this is just a girl, isn't it? Even if you say she looks like a Greek goddess, she's still only flesh and blood.

TCHAIK: *(Looking at his watch.)* What time do you make it?

TED: *(Takes wine from shopping bag and puts it in the icebox.)* Seven thirty just gone.

TCHAIK: Do you think she's not coming˜

TED: *(Reenters and stands at foot of bed.)* Of course she's coming. It's a free dinner, isn't it? I hope you've put clean sheets on this bed.

TCHAIK: What for? Oh, Ted, I wish you'd stop talking like that. *(Crosses onto balcony to replace cloth.)*

TED: *(Takes out a pack of Gaulloises and lights one.)* Look. Let's get things a bit clear. You go to hundreds of concerts. This is the first time you've picked up a bird and invited her home for fried chicken and vino, isn't it?

TCHAIK: *(Left of table — ties one shoe.)* I didn't pick her up. She was sitting next to me and dropped her program.

TED: On purpose.

TCHAIK: *(Crosses downstage center.)* Don't be silly. She's not the sort.

TED: Everyone's the sort.

TCHAIK: Well, she isn't. I just know. *(To front of table, and ties other shoe.)*

TED: *(Crosses to below stool.)* Well what's so wrong if she did? She wanted to get to know you. It's just possible, you know, that someone might want to get to know you.

TCHAIK: *(Uncomfortably.)* Don't be daft.

TED: *(Softer.)* You might try believing that, Tchaik. *(A tiny pause.)*

TCHAIK: *(Pours himself a glass of water.)* In any case, I didn't pick her up. That's a ridiculous expression, anyway. Sort of suggests weight-lifting.

TED: *(Sits on stool.)* What did you do then?

TCHAIK: *(Crosses to dresser.)* Well, I asked her if she liked music. It was a daft question really, because she wouldn't have been at a concert otherwise, would she? It turned out that she was on her own, so I asked her to have a coffee with me after. I could hardly believe it when she said yes. *(Takes a drink.)*

TED: Why not? Even goddesses get thirsty.

TCHAIK: We went to an Espresso bar in Kensington.

TED: And held hands under the table?

TCHAIK: *(Crosses center and sits in armchair.)* Not exactly. As a matter of fact, I couldn't think of anything to say to her. We just sat there for a little while and then left.

TED: So that's why you asked me here tonight? To help out with the talk?

TCHAIK: Well, you know what to say to women. You've had the practice.

TED: There's no practice needed. Just keep it going, that's all. Bright and not too filthy. The main thing is to edge it subtly towards where you want it to go. You know. In your case you'll be able to start off with music. *(He edges stool closer to the chair.)* "What a nice concert that was." *(Still closer.)* "I do like Mozart so much, don't you?" Then if she's got any sense at all she'll say, "Oh, yes, he does things to me!" and you'll say, *(This time the stool ends up right next to the chair.)* "What kind of things?" — and you're off to the races then, aren't you? *(He rises and crosses center.)* I'll give you a tip that usually works a treat. After a couple of hours, if she asks for a cigarette, don't give it to her; light it in your mouth and then hand it to her. *(He demonstrates.)* It's very intimate.

TCHAIK: I don't smoke.

TED: *(Crosses upstage center onto balcony.)* Well, you'll have to work out your own style, of course.

TCHAIK: What's it matter? She's not coming anyway.

TED: *(Sarcastic.)* Of course not.

TCHAIK: I mean it. Look at the time. It's nearly quarter to. She's thought better of it, I bet you.

TED: *(On balcony.)* Oh, don't be silly. Most girls think it's chic to be a little late. They think it makes them more desirable. It's only a trick.

TCHAIK: No, that's not her. She doesn't play tricks. That's why all that stuff is so silly — all this plotting. I say this, and she says that. I think things should just happen between people.

TED: *(Crosses downstage center to right of* TCHAIK.) Oh, yes. And how many times have they just happened with you?

TCHAIK: Well, that depends on what you want to happen.

TED: You know bloody well what you want to happen. *(Crosses to stool, kicks it back to its original position, and sits.)*

TCHAIK: *(Urgently.)* I don't. I don't. I don't. This isn't the sort of girl you can make plots about. It would be all wrong. Because she's sort of inaccessible. Pure — but not cold. Very warm.

TED: And you know all this after ten minutes' silence in a coffee bar?

TCHAIK: *(Rises and puts glass on table.)* You can know things like that without talking. She's not a talker — she's a listener. That can be more profound, you know. And she's got a look about her — not how people are, but how they ought to be. Do you know when I said that about a goddess, do you know who I was thinking of? Her.

TED: Venus?

TCHAIK: She's got exactly the same neck — long and gentle. That's a sign.

TED: What of?

TCHAIK: Spiritual beauty. Like Venus. *(Crosses to shelf downstage right for book and back again to center.)* That's what the picture really represents. The birth of beauty in the human soul. My Botticelli book says so. Listen. *(Reading from a Fontana pocket book.)* "Venus, that is to say humanity, is a nymph of excellent comeliness, born of heaven. Her soul and mind are Love and Charity. Her eyes, dignity. Her hands, liberality. Her feet, modesty." All signs, you see. "Venus is the mother of Grace, of Beauty, and of Faith."

TED: And this bird of yours is the mother of all that?

TCHAIK: *(Sits armchair.)* No, of course not. Stop trying to make me into a fool. What I mean is, that look of hers is ideal beauty. It means she's got grace inside her. Really beautiful people are beautiful inside them. Do you see?

TED: You mean like after taking Andrew's Liver Salts?

TCHAIK: *(Rising and replacing book downstage right.)* Yes, that's exactly what I mean.

TED: Oh, Tchaik, now seriously, come off it. That's all a lot of balls, and you know it. There's a lot of dim, greedy little nitty girls about who are as pretty as pictures.

TCHAIK: *(Puts Mozart record in sleeve.)* I don't mean pretty. I mean . . . well, what you called carriage, for instance. What your Lavinia's got. It's not just something you learn, the way to walk and that. It's something inside you. I mean real carriage, the way you see some girls walk, sort of putting the air around them like clothes — you can't practice that. You've got first to love the world. Then it comes out. *(Puts sleeve in record jacket. Tiny pause.)*

TED: *(Rising.)* You poor nut.

TCHAIK: What do you mean? *(Puts record jacket on shelf.)*

TED: Nut. Nut.

TCHAIK: Why?

TED: Oh, dear for you.

> *(The doorbell rings.)*

TCHAIK: God! There she is.

> *(TCHAIK rushes to the wardrobe for his blazer. Ted picks up towel, robe, and slippers from the bed. TCHAIK crosses to door — TED to wardrobe — they collide upstage center. TED throws towel, robe, slippers into the wardrobe. He turns and sees the tags on the blazer, runs to TCHAIK and rips them off.)*

TED: Now listen. Last swallow of coffee and I'm away. Cleaning tag! Nine thirty you'll see me. Nine thirty-one you won't. Work to do at home — get it? *(TCHAIK exits.)* Oh, hey — where's the bottle of Dubonnet? *(TCHAIK, reenters speechless.)* It's the one thing I left you to do.

TCHAIK: I know. I forgot.

TED: You nit! Now you've nothing to give her for a cocktail.

> *(The bell rings again.)*

TCHAIK: What am I going to do?

TED: Well, there's nothing you can do, is there? Just don't mention it, that's all. Say nothing about it. She comes from the suburbs. She probably won't expect anything. Wine at dinner will impress her enough.

TCHAIK: Oh, hell.

TED: Why don't you leave her standing there. She'll go away in five minutes. *(He pushes TCHAIK out of the door.)*

Take a Giant Step

by Louis Peterson

The Play

A young black boy is emerging from childhood into a bewildering adult world. He senses a growing estrangement from his white playmates and is expelled from school for standing up to a racist history teacher. Lonely and confused, he runs away and ends up in a saloon, where he is propositioned by a harlot. Feeling defeated, he returns home and receives an unforgiving scolding which causes him to become ill. His grandmother, a semi-invalid, comes to his defense. She maintains that the boy must have racial pride and that his parents should support him in the lonely pursuit of it. In the end, after his grandmother's death, he has resolved his problems. He doesn't need the companionship of the white boys in the neighborhood; he's going on with his music and his studies and he will go on to college.

The Scene

Spence has just been expelled from school. He is getting ready to run away from home when his best friend, Iggie, comes over to trade stamps with him.

SPENCE: Dear, dear God — if that's my mother, just kill me as I open the door. *(Crosses to door. He hides suitcase Left of piano. Opens door.)* Hi! Iggie — did you give me a scare!

IGGIE: Hiya, Spence.

SPENCE: I'm in a terrible hurry, Iggie. What do you want?

IGGIE: I just came over to see if you have any stamps to trade.

SPENCE: *(Crosses Left, gets shoes.)* I haven't got much time. Come on in — but you can't stay long. I've got to go somewhere.

IGGIE: *(Comes in.)* Where are you going?

SPENCE: No place. *(Pause.)* You sure you came over to trade stamps?

IGGIE: *(At sofa.)* Sure — that's what I came over for. I finished my homework early — and so I thought I might —

SPENCE: *(Sits in chair Left of table.)* You know, Iggie — you're going to be out of school for a week. You didn't have to get your homework done so soon. That's the most disgusting thing I ever heard.

IGGIE: *(Crosses to table.)* Now look, if I want to get my homework done — that's my business. I don't tell you it's disgusting when you don't get yours done at all, do I?

SPENCE: *(Crosses back to sofa.)* O.K. — O.K., Iggie. I only thought you came over because you heard I got kicked out of school.

IGGIE: No, Spence — I hadn't heard.

SPENCE: You're sure?

IGGIE: I told you I hadn't heard, didn't I? *(Sits Right of table.)*

SPENCE: *(Crosses Right to close door.)* That kind of news has a way of getting around. *(Looking at him.)* Well, what are you thinking about? *(Crosses back to sofa.)*

IGGIE: Nothing. I was just thinking that if I got kicked out of school, I guess I'd just as soon I dropped dead right there on the floor in the principal's office.

SPENCE: O.K., Iggie. You don't need to rub it in. I get the picture. *(Looks upstairs.)*

IGGIE: I'm sorry, Spence. Is there anything I can do?

SPENCE: Now, Iggie — pardon me for being so damn polite — but what in the hell could you do about it?

IGGIE: I only want to help, Spence.

SPENCE: *(Crosses Left to below table.)* Well, you can't — so let's drop it, shall we?

IGGIE: I didn't mean that business about dropping dead. I probably wouldn't drop dead anyway. There's nothing wrong with my heart.

SPENCE: *(Sits sofa.)* Iggie — will you please cut it out.

IGGIE: Anything you say. I didn't mean to offend you.

SPENCE: You didn't offend me, Iggie. You just talk too much — that's all.

IGGIE: I'll try to do better in the future.

SPENCE: Look, Iggie — I've gone and hurt your feelings — haven't I? Hell — I'm sorry. I've always liked you, Iggie. You're a good kid. I'm apologizing, Iggie.

IGGIE: It's O.K., Spence. I know you're upset.

SPENCE: *(Crosses down Left.)* I know how sensitive you are and all that and I just mow into you like crazy. I wish someone would tell me to shut my mouth. *(He walks to the stairs.)* Gram — hurry up with that dough, will you. Iggie — look — I'll tell you what I'm going to do for you. *(He goes over to the piano and comes back with his stamp album.)* Here — Iggie it's yours. I want you to have it — because you're my friend.

IGGIE: Your album! But don't you want it, Spence?

SPENCE: No, Iggie. I don't want it.

IGGIE: But why? I think you must be crazy. *(Stands.)*

SPENCE: Hell, Iggie — because I'm growing up. I'm becoming a man, Iggie. And since I'm going out in just a few minutes with my girl friend — you know it's time for me to quit fooling around with stuff like that.

IGGIE: Have you got a girl friend?

SPENCE: Yeh! Yes — I have — as a matter of fact I might get married soon. Forget all about school and all.

IGGIE: Really. Who is the girl, Spence?

SPENCE: Just a girl — that's all. And if everything works out O.K., I won't be coming back. You know, I'll have to get a job and stuff like that. Now you've got to go, Iggie, cause I've got to finish packing and get dressed. *(Leads IGGIE Center.)*

IGGIE: Where are you going, Spence?

SPENCE: I can't tell you, Iggie.

IGGIE: Are you sure you're feeling all right?

SPENCE: Yes, Iggie, I'm feeling all right.

IGGIE: *(Crossing to door.)* Thank you for the gift. I appreciate it.

SPENCE: Forget it.

IGGIE: It's a beautiful album.

SPENCE: It certainly is.

IGGIE: *(Crosses to Center.)* Hey, I was just thinking — maybe I could go up and talk to old Hasbrook. It might do some good.

SPENCE: *(Crosses to door.)* I don't care about that any more, Iggie. I'm pretty sure I won't be coming back to school.

IGGIE: Are you sure you want me to have this, Spence?

SPENCE: Yes, Iggie, I want you to have it.

IGGIE: *(Crossing to door.)* Well — I hope I'll see you soon. *(He is opening the door.)*

SPENCE: *(At door.)* Hey, Iggie! You won't mind if just once in a while — I come over and see how you're doing with it?

IGGIE: I hope you will. Goodbye. *(Exits.)*

SPENCE: Geez — I don't know what's wrong with me. I think maybe my brains are molding or something. *(Gets suitcase, shoves clothes inside and runs upstairs.)* Hey, Gram — will you hurry up with that five bucks so I can get the hell out of here before I really do something desperate!

Part 2: ADVANCED SCENES

Butterflies Are Free
by Leonard Gershe

The Play

Don Baker is an attractive young musician living in his own apartment in New York City for the first time. A pretty young actress (Jill) moves in next door. She proposes friendship and the removal of the connecting door. All the pieces are set up for a romance to begin. Well into the play, the audience and the actress find out that Don is blind. He is escaping from an overprotective mother and trying to learn if he has the talent to become a songwriter. Jill cannot deal with Don's blindness or her feelings for him and ends the relationship.

The Scene

Jill comes into Don's apartment to say good-bye and drop off the key to the door that adjoins their apartments. She is moving in with Ralph, the director. Don, who is in love with Jill, confronts her about her reasons for leaving and her inability to commit to their relationship.

JILL: *(Opens the door and enters carrying two suitcases. Setting the bags down by* D. L. *post.)* I think I made it. Listen, I left those new dish towels there . . . and the light bulbs, if you want them.
DON: I don't need them.
JILL: Well . . . I'll donate them to the apartment. Oh, and here's the key. *(Takes a key from her pocket, crosses below to coffee table*

and sets it down.) I'll leave it here on the table. Will you give it to
the super? *(Crosses up to apartment door.)* I guess you'd better
have him lock this door again.

DON: I'll wait and see who moves in. It might be someone groovy.

JILL: Oh. Yeah. I hope so. Well . . . let's don't have a big good-bye or
anything. I'll be seeing you.

DON: *(Crosses to ladder.)* Can't you stay a minute?

JILL: Well . . . once I'm going somewhere, I like to get going. You
know what I mean? *(Picks up bags.)*

DON: *(Crosses to D. R. post.)* I'm the same way. I was just going to
have a corned beef sandwich on rye. Want one?

JILL: *(Crosses through kitchen to front door.)* Once I'm going somewhere, I like to get going — *(Puts bags down by edge of platform.)* unless someone offers me a corned beef sandwich on rye.

DON: *(Crosses to refrigerator.)* How about a beer?

JILL: Sure. *(Crosses to above dining table.)* The candles are still lit.

DON: *(As he fixes sandwich and beer.)* I know. *(Closes refrigerator
door; crosses to counter with beer, gets glass, pours.)* I'm very religious.

JILL: Where's Mama?

DON: She went home.

JILL: I didn't hear her leave. What was the verdict?

DON: *(Holds glass out to JILL.)* She accepted my declaration of inde-
pendence.

JILL: *(Takes glass from DON.)* You're kidding!

DON: *(Crosses to refrigerator, gets sandwich.)* I gotta hand it to her —
she put up a great battle.

JILL: *(Crosses D. end of sofa.)* Maybe she should've won. I
mean . . . maybe you would be better off at home.

DON: *(Closes refrigerator door, crosses to counter, sandwich on
plate.)* That's a switch!

JILL: I've been thinking about it.

DON: Come on, girl. It took me a whole day and three pints of blood to
convince my mother. I don't want to have to start on you.

JILL: *(Crosses between coffee table and director's chair to U. end of
sofa.)* I like to have things done for me.

DON: Then give up Ralph and the play and move in with my mother.
I'm out of mustard. *(Moves down, slightly disoriented, and bumps
into post D. L.)*

JILL: *(Sits U. end of sofa, not looking at DON.)* I don't care. What do
you think of Ralph?

DON: *(Looking up, surprised.)* Where are you?

JILL: I'm on the sofa.

DON: Oh. I couldn't figure where your voice was coming from.

JILL: You always could before.

DON: *(Backs U. Handing her the plate.* JILL *takes it and puts it on table.)* I . . . I wasn't concentrating. *(Crosses up into kitchen counter.)* He seemed very nice.

JILL: Who?

DON: Ralph.

JILL: You didn't like him, did you?

DON: I said he seemed very nice.

JILL: I could tell you didn't like him. You were a little uptight when he was here.

DON: *(Crosses above table to D. L. post.)* I'm always a little uptight when there's more than one person in the room. I have to figure out who's speaking, and if he's speaking to me.

JILL: I guess you didn't like him because he was rude.

DON: *(Holds onto D. L. post.)* Was he rude?

JILL: Well, you know, putting down Scarsdale like that to your mother.

DON: That was an accident. He didn't know she was from Scarsdale. I'm sorry you think he's rude.

JILL: I don't think he's rude.

DON: Well, you said it. I didn't. Or is there someone else here?

JILL: *(Rises, crosses above director's chair.)* I know he comes off as a little conceited.

DON: Tell me, Jill, do *you* like Ralph?

JILL: *(With a self-conscious laugh.)* What kind of a question is that? I'm moving in with him, aren't I? Why would I move in with a guy I didn't like?

DON: That was my next question.

JILL: *(Crosses to bags.)* I'd better be going. . . .

DON: *(Quickly. Crosses off platform, grabs D. arm of sofa.)* Come to think of it, I guess I don't like Ralph.

JILL: *(Crosses U. end of sofa.)* I knew it all along. But why?

DON: *(Sits D. end of sofa.)* Like you said — he's rude and conceited.

JILL: *(Crosses between coffee table and director's chair.)* But I've been trying to tell you he's not like that. I knew that's what you thought, but he's not at all conceited.

DON: And thanks a lot for making me feel his face.

JILL: I thought you might like him better if you knew what he looked like. He's got a good face.

DON: To look at, maybe, but it doesn't come across to the touch.

JILL: *(Crosses away* R. *a step or two.)* I'm sorry about that. I hoped we could all be friends. *(Crosses to bags.)* Well, I'd better . . .

DON: *(Quickly.)* You know something? I'm going to tell you something. YOU don't like Ralph.

JILL: Oh, God!! I just packed two suitcases which are sitting right over there so I can move in with him!!

DON: I don't care if you have thirteen trunks! You don't like him.

JILL: *(Crosses through kitchen to above table* C.) Boy, you really are too much! You think just because you're blind you can see everything!!

DON: That's right — that sixth sense we've got tells me you don't like Ralph Austin! How about that? Spooky, isn't it?

JILL: *(Crosses through kitchen to* U. C.) No, it's just stupid. I have two bags which are packed and sitting right there . . .

DON: Tell me — with Ralph, is it like the Fourth of July and like Christmas?

JILL: Not exactly . . . but he has a kind of strength. With him it's more like — Labor Day.

DON: Do you think *he's* a beautiful person, too?

JILL: In many ways, yes.

DON: Has he got charisma?

JILL: Definitely!

DON: Then I'm selling mine.

JILL: *(Crosses* U. *end of coffee table.)* You'd better hurry. It's been known to fade away.

DON: Do you love him?

JILL: Why should I answer that? No matter what I say, you've already made up your own mind.

DON: *(Rises.)* Go ahead, answer it! Do you love him?!

JILL: Yes! In my way.

DON: This morning you told me you could never love anyone.

JILL: *(Crosses* D. L. *through kitchen to* R. *of director's chair.)* That was this morning. Am I allowed to change my mind or has my first statement already been passed into law by Congress?!

DON: *(Crosses* D.) Look, I'm not the worldliest human being on the block, but I know that when you're rushing into the arms of the man you love, you don't stop for a corned beef sandwich on rye.

JILL: (DON *turns toward her voice.)* Which shows how little you know me. Some people wear their hearts on their sleeves . . . . I wear my appetite.

DON: *(Crosses to D. R. post, bumps into stool on the* way.*)* Was it something my mother said?

JILL: *(Backs away R.)* Was what something your mother said?

DON: The reason you're leaving. The reason you didn't show up for dinner. I know you didn't forget. Was it something my mother said?

JILL: *You* don't even listen to your mother. Why should I?

DON: Then why are you leaving? And don't give me that crap about loving Ralph.

JILL: *(Crossing below* DON U. *between coffee table and sofa.)* I'm leaving because I want to leave. I'm free and I go when I want to go.

DON: *(Crosses to ladder, hangs onto it, faces away from her.)* I thought it might have something to do with me.

JILL: *(Sits C. sofa.)* It has nothing whatsoever to do with you.

DON: Okay. You're scared to death of becoming involved, aren't you?

JILL: I don't want to get involved. I told you that.

DON: *(Turns toward* JILL.*)* That's right — you told me. No commitments . . . no responsibility.

JILL: I have to be able to get out if I get tired of the . . .

DON: Tired of me?

JILL: Anybody!

DON: What if I got tired of you?

JILL: *(This hadn't occurred to her.)* Of me??

DON: Doesn't anyone ever get tired of you?

JILL: I don't hang around long enough to find out.

DON: *(Crosses above director's chair.)* With Ralph, you could get out any time you feel like it . . . but it might be harder to walk out on a blind guy, right?

JILL: The blindness has nothing to do with it. Nothing!

DON: *(Crosses to U. end of coffee table.* JILL *crouches in D. corner of sofa.)* You know goddam well it has! You wouldn't feel a thing walking out on Ralph or Sebastian or Irving, but if you walked out on Little Donny Dark, you might hate yourself and you wouldn't like that, would you?! Hate *me* — or love *me* — but don't leave because I'm blind and don't stay because I'm blind!!

JILL: Who are Sebastian and Irving?

DON: *(Crosses D. R. post.)* Nobody. I made them up.

JILL: Sometimes I don't understand you. *(Crosses above director's chair.)* We don't think alike and I know I'd only hurt you sooner or later. I don't want to hurt you.

DON: Why not? You do it to everybody else. Why do I rate special treatment?

JILL: I don't want to be another Linda Fletcher. She hurt you, didn't she?

DON: She helped me, too. She was there when I needed her.

JILL: *(Steps in to him.)* I can't promise that. I don't know where I'll be when you need me.

DON: *(Turns away from her.)* You need me a helluva lot more than I need you!

JILL: I don't need anybody. I never did and I never will. *(Crosses to bags.)* I have to go now.

DON: I'm glad you said *have* to and not *want* to.

JILL: Boy, I finally said something right. I'll be seeing you.

DON: *(Turns front.)* Yeah — I'll be seeing you. I'll think about you for years and wonder if you ever made a commitment . . . if you ever got involved.

JILL: I hope not.

DON: Don't worry. It won't happen *(Crosses between director's chair and coffee table to D. L.)* because you're emotionally retarded. Did you know that? That's why you couldn't face marriage. It's why you can't face anything permanent . . . anything real. You're leaving now because you're afraid you might fall in love with me . . . and you're too adolescent for that responsibility . . . and you're going to stay that way. Oh God, I feel sorry for you . . . because you're crippled. I'd rather be blind. (JILL *exits, closing the door behind her. He turns, crosses to the table and starts to clear D. setting. A fork drops to the floor. DON tries to figure out where the sound came from, then takes the plate and puts it in the sink. Suddenly, he crosses to his tape recorder and turns it on. We hear the last part of his song as he crosses to kitchen, stumbling into a stool. He goes to the dining table and blows out the candles. His hand touches the flowers. With quiet anger, he crushes the flowers in a tight fist, then grabs cloth and pulls it off the table, knocking other things to the floor along with it. He crosses L. toward the living room. He bumps into the D. stool. He tosses it upstage out of his way. He stumbles against the D. S. edge of the sofa and falls to the floor. He lies on the floor by coffee table with tears filling his eyes and no interest in getting up. The front door opens. JILL enters carrying her bags. She sets her bags down and looks around the room for DON. When she sees him, a look of pain comes to her face.* DON *sits up, quickly, aware of someone in the room.)* Who is it? Who's there?

JILL: *(Breaking the tension. Crosses* C.*)* The news is good. It's not your mother.

DON: What are you doing here?

JILL: *(Crosses to him, sits beside him, takes his hand and kisses it.)* What are you doing on the floor?

DON: I was about to have a picnic.

JILL: What a great idea!!

(DON starts to laugh with JILL. *He reaches out for her. She goes into his arms and they cling together, laughing.)*

(One Female and One Male)

Lu Ann Hampton Laverty Oberlander
by Preston S. Jones

The Play

Lu Ann Hampton, a seventeen-year-old high school cheerleader who lives in a small town in West Texas called Bradleyville, dreams of traveling to faraway places. She settles down and marries a friend of her Korean War veteran brother, only to divorce him ten years later and take a job as a beauty technician. Lu Ann meets Corky Oberlander, marries him soon after, only to lose him quickly in an automobile accident. The play fast forwards another ten years, where we find Lu Ann still in Bradleyville with her teenaged daughter, her alcoholic brother, and her stroke-enfeebled mother. This is when she is unexpectedly visited by her high school sweetheart, who has become a successful preacher.

The Scene

This is the first scene in the play. Lu Ann, a cheerleader, is coming home from the pep rally at school with her boyfriend, Billy Bob. Billy Bob and the rest of the basketball team dyed their hair green for the school assembly.

BILLY BOB: *(Offstage.)* Lu Ann! Lu Ann! Wait up, will ya! *(Following* LU ANN *on.* BILLY BOB WORTMAN *is tall and lanky. He wears a white shirt, Levi's, boots, and a letter sweater. His crew-cut hair has been dyed green.)*

LU ANN: Ma! I'm home!

[CLAUDINE: *(Offstage.)* About time!]

LU ANN: Well, ah thought ah would die! Ah jest thought ah would curl up and die right there on the gym floor. When the coach introduced the basketball team and you-all come out there with your hair all dyed green. Well, sir, mah eyes liked to jumped plumb outta mah head! Why, Mary Beth Johnson jest hollered. That's right, jest hollered right out loud.

BILLY BOB: It was Pete Honeycutt's idea.

LU ANN: Why ever'one jest laughed and shouted and carried on so. Eveline Blair came runnin' over to me shoutin', "Look at the basketball boys, look at the basketball boys!"

BILLY BOB: It was Pete Honeycutt's idea.

LU ANN: *(Gestures to porch — they go out.)* After the assembly we cheerleaders all got together and decided we'd do somethin' funny too.

BILLY BOB: Aw, like what?

LU ANN: Now wouldn't you like to know? Mr. Green-headed Billy Bob Wortman.

BILLY BOB: Aw, come on, Lu Ann, what are you-all fixin' to do?

LU ANN: Oh, ah don't know, somethin', somethin' real neat.

BILLY BOB: You cain't dye you-all's hair. Pete Honeycutt already thought that one up.

LU ANN: Eveline Blair thought up different shoes.

BILLY BOB: Different shoes?

LU ANN: You know, come to school wearin' one high-heel shoe and one saddle shoe. Somethin' *neato* like that.

BILLY BOB: Yeah.

LU ANN: Ah don't know, though, it might be kinda tricky doin' the Locomotive in a high-heel shoe.

BILLY BOB: Might be at that.

LU ANN: But it might be fun.

BILLY BOB: Shore.

LU ANN: *(Sitting on swing.)* Maybe we can wear them out to the senior picnic.

BILLY BOB: *(Joins her.)* Shore!

LU ANN: We're still goin' in your daddy's Hudson, ain't we?

BILLY BOB: Well, uh, naw, we gotta use the pickup.

LU ANN: The pickup!

BILLY BOB: Yeah, my dad wants the car to go over to Big Spring.

LU ANN: But it's the senior picnic! Mah God, ah don't want to go to mah one and only senior picnic in a danged-old pickup.

BILLY BOB: Well, goshalmighty, Lu Ann, ah cain't help it.

LU ANN: What the heck good is it for your dad to have a bran'-new, step-down Hudson Hornet if we never get to use the danged old thing.

BILLY BOB: Seems like ever'thin' ah do is wrong.

LU ANN: Boy, that's the truth.

BILLY BOB: Gawlee, Ruthie Lee Lawell and Pete Honeycutt are goin' in his pickup.

LU ANN: So what.

BILLY BOB: Well, nuthin', ah jest mean that it don't seem to bother Ruthie Lee none.

LU ANN: Heck no, it don't bother Ruthie Lee none. Mah Gawd, she almost lives in Pete Honeycutt's pickup seat. I'll bet her bra spends more time on the danged gear shift than it spends on her.

BILLY BOB: *(Shocked.)* Lu Ann Hampton! You know that ain't true.

LU ANN: It is so, too. I seen 'em when they was parked out to the drive-in and she was danged near naked.

BILLY BOB: I never saw nuthin'.

LU ANN: 'Course you never saw nuthin'. You was too busy watchin' the movie. Mah Gawd, you was more worried about old Gary Cooper than Grace Kelly was.

BILLY BOB: Ah liked that movie.

LU ANN: Boy, you shore did.

BILLY BOB: Well, ah did.

LU ANN: No wonder Ruthie has so many chest colds in the wintertime.

BILLY BOB: If Pete and Ruthie Lee was actin' like the way you said, that jest means they don't have respect for each other.

LU ANN: Or for Gary Cooper.

BILLY BOB: Reverend Stone says that goin' on like that is a sinful sign of no respect.

LU ANN: Oh, brother.

BILLY BOB: People that behave thataway out to drive-ins and suchlike is behavin' plumb unChristian.

LU ANN: Well, at least they were sharin' somethin' more that a danged ol' box of popcorn.

BILLY BOB: A true Christian is pure in mind and body.

LU ANN: I wish you'd stop preachin', Billy Bob. Mah Gawd, ever' time we have somethin' important to discuss, you come up with a danged sermon.

BILLY BOB: What in the world are we discussin' that's important?

LU ANN: Your daddy's step-down Hudson Hornet, that's what!

BILLY BOB: My daddy's . . . For cryin' out loud, Lu Ann, sometimes you drive me absolutely nuts!

LU ANN: Well, you don't have to yell, Billy Bob.

BILLY BOB: Ah told you, an' told you, an' told you that we cain't have the Hudson.

LU ANN: Well, why not?

BILLY BOB: 'Cause my daddy's got to go over to Big Spring!

LU ANN: Well, it seems plumb funny to me that your daddy picked the very day of the senior picnic to go over to Big Spring. Ah mean, doesn't he know that the senior picnic is jest about the most important event in our whole schoolin' career?

BILLY BOB: Ah don't know if he does or not, he jest . . .

LU ANN: Don't hardly seem fair to look forward to somethin' all these years only to have your daddy come along and mess it up.

BILLY BOB: Daddy ain't messed up nothin', he jest . . .

LU ANN: He's only doin' it for spite, Billy Bob.

BILLY BOB: No, he ain't, he's jest . . .

LU ANN: And spite in my book is jest plain sinful and un-Christian. *(She turns to go.)* Good night, Billy Bob.

BILLY BOB: *(Grabbing her arm.)* Now wait a minute, Lu Ann. *(They are very close now.)* Oh, boy, uh, uh. Ah will talk to Dad tonight and ask for the car again, okay?

LU ANN: Swell, Billy Bob. *(She kisses him.)* Good night, now.

BILLY BOB: Good night. By gollies, Lu Ann, ah'm gonna make danged sure we git that car.

LU ANN: Fine.

BILLY BOB: Danged sure! *(He exits.)*

(LU ANN watches him for a moment and then enters the house.)

(One Female and One Male)

The Stonewater Rapture
by Doug Wright

The Play

The play tells the story of two teenagers whose sexual awakening has been severely hampered by their fundamentalist religious background. Concerned with the explosive combination of adolescent sexuality and religious repression in a rural Texas town, the play traces the relationship between Whitney, the son of the local minister, and Carlyle, an eighteen-year-old girl with a highly charged imagination.

The Scene

Set on the front porch and living room of Whitney's home, the scene details Whitney's attempt to seduce the God-fearing Carlyle.

WHITNEY: Are we going out together or what?
CARLYLE: What do you mean?
WHITNEY: You're here every night, or I'm at your house, we study together, now we're on the Youth Ministry, and we've never even kissed.
CARLYLE: *(Embarrassed.)* Whitney . . .
WHITNEY: That makes us abnormal by most standards.
CARLYLE: But I —
WHITNEY: Sort of reverse perverted.

CARLYLE: *(Rolling her eyes.)* You can kiss me. *(She offers her cheek.)*

WHITNEY: You're not my grandmother.

CARLYLE: You can kiss me on the lips if you'll sit on your hands.

WHITNEY: What?

CARLYLE: Or go hungry. *(*WHITNEY *sits on his hands and kisses* CARLYLE. *She submits for a moment, then pulls back suddenly, and blurts.)* Mrs. Maxwell found out I made all A's in art, so she put me in charge of all the decorations for the pep rallies and the football parties. Arthur Horrishill's having a party at his father's barn tomorrow night, but it's not school sponsored and there may not be chaperones. He wants me to do the decorations, and it sure would be good practice. But I'm not sure I should go if there aren't going to be chaperones. What do you think?

WHITNEY: Can I kiss you again?

CARLYLE: Yes. *(They do.)* You moved your hand.

WHITNEY: I know.

CARLYLE: Take it off.

WHITNEY: Move it.

CARLYLE: Please.

WHITNEY: If you really like me, you'll do me a big favor.

CARLYLE: I said take it off, not move it up.

WHITNEY: I think it has a mind of its own!

CARLYLE: NO! *(*CARLYLE *forcefully pushes* WHITNEY*'s hand away.)*

WHITNEY: It's no different than when someone brushes up against you in the grocery store. That's not sinful. Pretend I'm reaching for the canned peaches, only I miss. *(As* WHITNEY *enacts the scenario, he places a hand on* CARLYLE*'s shoulder, her knee, etc.)* "Excuse me. In which aisle will I find the canned peaches? Seven? Ooh, thank-you. Canned apples, canned pears, canned cherries — ah, here we are — peaches!"

CARLYLE: *(Laughing.)* Stop it. No more.

WHITNEY: I want to make a whole fruit salad.

CARLYLE: *(With finality.)* Order out.

WHITNEY: Please, Carlyle. I need this.

CARLYLE: Nobody needs it, Whitney.

WHITNEY: Oh yeah? It's all I've been thinking about. For weeks. Years. Ever since sixth grade. I've lost sleep some nights because there isn't any blood to go to my brain. I can't concentrate on anything. I look at people crossing the street, and they're all naked. I look at cars, and I think of back seats. I look at this couch, and I know it folds out. It's driving me crazy.

CARLYLE: Mama lets me see you because she knows I'll be safe. You're not like Arthur Horrishill and Michael MaCaffey.

WHITNEY: I'm just like them, only not as brave.

CARLYLE: If Mama knew I let you kiss me, she'd kill me.

WHITNEY: We don't have to do anything, just let me put my hand there. Just once. For five seconds. You can time it.

CARLYLE: *(Weakly.)* I don't have a watch.

WHITNEY: You're not twelve years old! We're both eighteen, and we've never done a thing. Don't you think that's a bit weird?

CARLYLE: "It is good for a man not to touch a woman." That's First Corinthians, chapter seven, verse one.

WHITNEY: Don't be such a prude! I'm dead serious. This is hard for me. Unless I make a move soon, it's all gonna dry up and my chance will be over.

CARLYLE: Whitney . . .

WHITNEY: People make fun of me for it. Please. You're the only girl who even likes me. The others are all so eerie. When I'm around them, my whole mouth turns into Jell-O. I can talk to you. Sometimes I think you're my only friend.

CARLYLE: Well, you don't make it very easy. Sometimes they give me a pretty hard time about you.

WHITNEY: Who does?

CARLYLE: The girls. Saying all you do is make wisecracks and that sometimes you try too hard because you're nervous.

WHITNEY: They talk about me like that?

CARLYLE: So it's pretty nice of me to even be here. *(Silence.)* Aw, Whitney. I don't care what they say. They're silly. But don't do this to me.

WHITNEY: You're the only person I've ever gone out with. You know that. And I always pay for everything. We've never dutched. I think of how old I am, and I get scared.

CARLYLE: Five seconds. No more. (WHITNEY *places his hand on* CARLYLE's *breast.*) One. Two. Three. Four . . . *(She jerks away.)* I said you could put it there, I didn't say you could flex it!

WHITNEY: My palm itched.

CARLYLE: Try again. (WHITNEY *replaces his hand.*) One thousand. Two thousand. Three thousand. Four thousand. Five thousand. (WHITNEY *removes his hand.*) Was I counting fast?

WHITNEY: I'm not sure.

CARLYLE: You count. *(WHITNEY replaces his hand.)*
WHITNEY: One, one thousand . . . Two, one thousand . . . Three, one
   thousand . . . Four, one thousand . . . Five, one thousand . . . Six,
   one thousand . . . Seven, one thousand . . . Eight, one thousand . . . Nine, one thousand . . . Ten, one thousand . . . Eleven,
   one thousand . . . *(WHITNEY has pushed CARLYLE down on
   the couch, and with his free hand has opened his fly and is guid-
   ing her hand to his crotch. She runs her hand in and out across
   his thigh. Suddenly, she pulls back fiercely.)*
CARLYLE: DON'T! DON'T YOU DARE! *(CARLYLE bolts off the
   couch, and runs behind it.)* GOD IS NOT READY FOR ME TO
   FORNICATE!

A Taste of Honey

by Shelagh Delaney

The Play

Upon moving into a rundown flat with her teenage daughter, Helen, part-time prostitute and even lesser-time mother, is visited by Peter, one of her regulars. After Peter's marriage proposal, Helen takes off with him for the Christmas season leaving Jo, her teenage daughter, to fend for herself. Jo meets a black sailor who abandons her, leaving more than his engagement ring behind. A homosexual art student (Geof) takes care of Jo during her pregnancy while Peter, tiring of Helen, abandons her, resulting in the reuniting of mother and daughter.

The Scene

It is late afternoon and hot. Jo, miserable with her own life, is doing her best to provoke Geof. Geof is working on a dress for the baby and doing his best to keep this young mother-to-be in line.

JO: God! It's hot.
GEOF: I know it's hot.
JO: I'm so restless.
GEOF: Oh, stop prowling about.
JO: This place stinks. *(Goes over to the door. Children are heard singing in the street.)* That river, it's the colour of lead. Look at that washing, it's dirty, and look at those filthy children.
GEOF: It's not their fault.

JO: It's their parents' fault. There's a little boy over there and his hair, honestly, it's walking away. And his ears. Oh! He's a real mess! He never goes to school. He just sits on that front doorstep all day. I think he's a bit deficient.

    (The children's voices die away. A tugboat hoots.)

His mother ought not to be allowed.

GEOF: Who?

JO: His mother. Think of all the harm she does, having children.

GEOF: Sit down and read a book, Jo.

JO: I can't.

GEOF: Be quiet then. You're getting on my nerves. *(Suddenly she yells and whirls across the room.)*

JO: Wheee! Come on rain. Come on storm. It kicked me, Geof. It kicked me!

GEOF: What?

JO: It kicked me. *(GEOF runs to her and puts his head on her belly.)*

GEOF: Will it do it again?

JO: It shows it's alive anyway. Come on, baby, let's see what big sister's making for us.

GEOF: Put it down.

JO: What a pretty little dress.

GEOF: It's got to wear something. You can't just wrap it up in a bundle of newspaper.

JO: And dump it on a doorstep. How did Geoffrey find out the measurements?

GEOF: Babies are born to the same size more or less.

JO: Oh, no, they're not. Some are thin scrappy things and others are huge and covered in rolls of fat.

GEOF: Shut up, Jo, it sounds revolting.

JO: They are revolting. I hate babies.

GEOF: I thought you'd change. Motherhood is supposed to come natural to women.

JO: It comes natural to you, Geoffrey Ingram. You'd make somebody a wonderful wife. What were you talking about to that old mare downstairs?

GEOF: I was giving her the rent. I got my grant yesterday.

JO: You're as thick as thieves, you two.

GEOF: She's going to make the baby a cradle.

JO: What?

GEOF: You know, she makes wicker baskets.

JO: A wicker basket!

GEOF: It's the best we can do, unless you want to go down to the river plaiting reeds.

JO: I don't want her poking her nose into my affairs.

GEOF: You're glad enough to have me dancing attendance on you.

JO: Only because I thought you'd leave me alone. Why don't you leave me alone? *(She cries and flings herself down on the couch.)* I feel like throwing myself in the river.

GEOF: I wouldn't do that. It's full of rubbish.

JO: Well that's all I am, isn't it?

GEOF: Stop pitying yourself.

JO: Don't jump down my throat.

GEOF: How much longer is this going on?

JO: What?

GEOF: Your present performance.

JO: Nobody asked you to stay here. You moved in on me, remember, remember? If you don't like it you can get out, can't you? But you wouldn't do that, would you, Geoffrey? You've no confidence in yourself, have you? You're afraid the girls might laugh . . .

GEOF: Read that book and shut up. When the baby comes, if it ever does, you won't know one end of it from the other.

JO: *Looking After Baby*. Isn't that nice? Three months, exercises, constipation. Four months, relaxation. It even tells you how to wash nappies. How lovely. There's a little job for you, Geoffrey.

GEOF: Drink that. *(He hands her a glass of milk.)*

JO: *(Flirting with him.)* Does it tell you how to feed babies, Geoffrey?

GEOF: Even you know that.

JO: I know about that way, breast feeding, but I'm not having a little animal nibbling away at me, it's cannibalistic. Like being eaten alive.

GEOF: Stop trying to be inhuman. It doesn't suit you.

JO: I mean it. I hate motherhood.

GEOF: Well, whether you hate it or not you've got it coming to you so you might as well make a good job of it.

JO: I've got a toothache.

GEOF: I've got bloody heartache!

JO: I think you'd like everybody to think this baby's yours, wouldn't you, Geoffrey?

GEOF: Not likely.

JO: After all, you don't show much sign of coming fatherhood, do you? You like babies, don't you, Geof?

GEOF: Yes, I do.

JO: *(Coquettes with him.)* Geoffrey, have you got any of that toothache cure?

    (He moves away.)

    Geoffrey, have you got any of that toothache cure?

GEOF: The only cure for the toothache is a visit to the dentist. Drink your milk.

JO: I hate milk *(She looks out of the window.)* I never thought I'd still be here in the summer. *(She puts her arms round* GEOF *playfully.)* Would you like to be the father of my baby, Geoffrey?

GEOF: Yes, I would.

    (JO stands in the doorway. The children can be heard singing again.)

    What time is it?

JO: Half-past four by the church clock. Why do you stay here, Geof?

GEOF: Someone's got to look after you. You can't look after yourself.

JO: I think there's going to be a storm. Look at that sky. It's nearly black. And you can hear the kids playing, right over there on the croft.

    (A silence in the room: we hear the children singing.)

GEOF: What would you say if I started something?

JO: Eh!

GEOF: I said what would you say if I started something?

JO: In my condition I'd probably faint.

GEOF: No, I mean after.

JO: I don't want you.

GEOF: Am I repulsive to you?

JO: You're nothing to me. I'm everything to myself.

GEOF: No, you're not. You're going to need me after.

JO: I won't be here after.

GEOF: Do you still think he might come back?

JO: I've forgotten him.

    (She turns towards him, he to her.)

GEOF: You do need me, Jo, don't you?

JO: Let go of me. You're squeezing my arm.

GEOF: I've never kissed a girl.

JO: That's your fault.

GEOF: Let me kiss you.

JO: Let go of me. Leave me alone.
>   *(She struggles but he kisses her.)*
GEOF: How was that for the first time?
JO: Practise on somebody else.
GEOF: I didn't mean to hurt you.
JO: Look Geof, I like you, I like you very much, but I don't enjoy all
>   this panting and grunting . . .
GEOF: Marry me, Jo.
JO: Don't breathe all over me like that, you sound like a horse. I'm not
>   marrying anybody.
GEOF: I wouldn't ask you to do anything you didn't want to do.
JO: Yes, you would.
GEOF: Jo, I don't mind that you're having somebody else's baby.
>   What you've done, you've done. What I've done, I've done.
JO: I like you, Geof, but I don't want to marry you.
GEOF: Oh, all right. Anyway, I don't suppose I could live up to that
>   black beast of a prince of yours. I bet you didn't struggle when he
>   made love to you.
JO: It might have been better if I had.
GEOF: *(He gives her a bar of chocolate.)* Have some chocolate.
JO: Thanks. Do you want some?
GEOF: No.
JO: Go on.
GEOF: I said no.
JO: You like strawberry cream.
GEOF: I don't want any, Jo. I've made my mind up.
JO: Don't be daft, have some chocolate.
GEOF: No . . . *(She gives a piece of chocolate to him just the same.)*
JO: I think it would be best if you left this place, Geof. I don't think it's
>   doing you any good being here with me all the time.
GEOF: I know that, but I couldn't go away now.
JO: You'll have to go some time. We can't stay together like this for
>   ever.
GEOF: I'd sooner be dead than away from you.
JO: You say that as if you mean it.
GEOF: I do mean it.
JO: Why?
GEOF: Before I met you I didn't care one way or the other — I didn't
>   care whether I lived or died. But now . . .
JO: I think I'll go and lie down. *(She goes to bed and lies across it.)*

GEOF: There's no need for me to go, Jo. You said yourself you didn't want anybody else here and I'm only interested in you. We needn't split up need we, Jo?

JO: I don't suppose so.

A View from the Bridge

by Arthur Miller

The Play

Eddie Carbone, a longshoreman of Italian descent, lives on the Brooklyn waterfront with his wife, Beatrice, and his orphaned niece, Catherine. He treats the eighteen-year-old girl like a child and believes he loves her like a daughter. Two of his wife's cousins, Marco and Rodolpho, are smuggled in illegally from Italy and Eddie gives them shelter. When Catherine falls in love with Rodolpho, Eddie is violently opposed to this romance and refuses to let go of Catherine. This opposition is not motivated, as he thinks, by a dislike of the boy and a suspicion that he is too pretty to be a man, but by his unconscious desire for Catherine. Eddie accuses Rodolpho of wanting to marry Catherine only in order to achieve American citizenship. When Eddie fails to convince Catherine and she agrees to marry Rodolpho, Eddie must deal with impulses that he barely understands. From these feelings springs an act of betrayal with tragic and shattering results.

The Scene

Eddie has warned Catherine that Rodolpho is marrying her in order to obtain his American citizenship. In this scene, Catherine, shaken by Eddie's claims, tests Rodolpho's love by asking him to move to Italy with her after their marriage.

114

Light is rising on CATHERINE *in the apartment.* RODOLPHO *is watching as she arranges a paper pattern on cloth spread on the table.*

CATHERINE: You hungry?

RODOLPHO: Not for anything to eat. Pause. I have nearly three hundred dollars. Catherine?

CATHERINE: I heard you.

RODOLPHO: You don't like to talk about it any more?

CATHERINE: Sure, I don't mind talkin' about it.

RODOLPHO: What worries you, Catherine?

CATHERINE: I been wantin' to ask you about something. Could I?

RODOLPHO: All the answers are in my eyes, Catherine. But you don't look in my eyes lately. You're full of secrets. *(She looks at him. She seems withdrawn.)* What is the question?

CATHERINE: Suppose I wanted to live in Italy.

RODOLPHO: *(Smiling at the incongruity.)* You going to marry somebody rich?

CATHERINE: No, I mean live there — you and me.

RODOLPHO: *(His smile vanishing.)* When?

CATHERINE: Well . . . when we get married.

RODOLPHO: *(Astonished.)* You want to be an Italian?

CATHERINE: No, but I could live there without being Italian. Americans live there.

RODOLPHO: Forever?

CATHERINE: Yeah.

RODOLPHO: *(Crosses to rocker.)* You're fooling.

CATHERINE: No, I mean it.

RODOLPHO: Where do you get such an idea?

CATHERINE: Well, you're always saying it's so beautiful there, with the mountains and the ocean and all the —

RODOLPHO: You're fooling me.

CATHERINE: I mean it.

RODOLPHO: *(Goes to her slowly.)* Catherine, if I ever brought you home with no money, no business, nothing, they would call the priest and the doctor and they would say Rodolpho is crazy.

CATHERINE: I know, but I think we would be happier there.

RODOLPHO: Happier! What would you eat? You can't cook the view!

CATHERINE: Maybe you could be a singer, like in Rome or —

RODOLPHO: Rome! Rome is full of singers.

CATHERINE: Well, I could work then.

RODOLPHO: Where?

CATHERINE: God, there must be jobs somewhere!

RODOLPHO: There's nothing! Nothing, nothing, nothing. Now tell me what you're talking about. How can I bring you from a rich country to suffer in a poor country? What are you talking about? *(She searches for words.)* I would be a criminal stealing your face. In two years you would have an old, hungry face. When my brother's babies cry they give them water, water that boiled a bone. Don't you believe that?

CATHERINE: *(Quietly.)* I'm afraid of Eddie here.

(Slight pause.)

RODOLPHO: *(Steps closer to her.)* We wouldn't live here. Once I am a citizen I could work anywhere and I would find better jobs and we would have a house, Catherine. If I were not afraid to be arrested I would start to be something wonderful here!

CATHERINE: *(Steeling herself.)* Tell me something. I mean just tell me, Rodolpho — would you still want to do it if it turned out we had to go live in Italy? I mean just if it turned out that way.

RODOLPHO: This is your question or his question?

CATHERINE: I would like to know, Rodolpho. I mean it.

RODOLPHO: To go there with nothing.

CATHERINE: Yeah.

RODOLPHO: No. *(She looks at him wide-eyed.)* No.

CATHERINE: You wouldn't?

RODOLPHO: No; I will not marry you to live in Italy. I want you to be my wife, and I want to be a citizen. Tell him that, or I will. Yes. *(He moves about angrily.)*

And tell him also, and tell yourself, please, that I am not a beggar, and you are not a horse, a gift, a favor for a poor immigrant.

CATHERINE: Well, don't get mad!

RODOLPHO: I am furious! *(Goes to her.)* Do you think I am so desperate? My brother is desperate, not me. You think I would carry on my back the rest of my life a woman I didn't love just to be an American? It's so wonderful? You think we have no tall buildings in Italy? Electric lights? No wide streets? No flags? No automobiles? Only work we don't have. I want to be an American so I can work, that is the only wonder here — work! How can you insult me, Catherine?

CATHERINE: I didn't mean that —

RODOLPHO: My heart dies to look at you. Why are you so afraid of him?

CATHERINE: *(Near tears.)* I don't know!

RODOLPHO: Do you trust me, Catherine? You?

CATHERINE: It's only that I — He was good to me, Rodolpho. You don't know him; he was always the sweetest guy to me. Good. He razzes me all the time but he don't mean it. I know. I would — just feel ashamed if I made him sad. 'Cause I always dreamt that when I got married he would be happy at the wedding, and laughin' — and now he's — mad all the time and nasty — *(She is weeping.)* Tell him you'd live in Italy — just tell him, and maybe he would start to trust you a little, see? Because I want him to be happy; I mean — I like him, Rodolpho — and I can't stand it!

RODOLPHO: Oh, Catherine — oh, little girl.

CATHERINE: I love you, Rodolpho, I love you.

RODOLPHO: Then why are you afraid? That he'll spank you?

CATHERINE: Don't, don't laugh at me! I've been here all my life. . . . Every day I saw him when he left in the morning and when he came home at night. You think it's so easy to turn around and say to a man he's nothin' to you no more?

RODOLPHO: I know, but —

CATHERINE: You don't know; nobody knows! I'm not a baby, I know a lot more than people think I know. Beatrice says to be a woman, but —

RODOLPHO: Yes.

CATHERINE: Then why don't she be a woman? If I was a wife I would make a man happy instead of goin' at him all the time. I can tell a block away when he's blue in his mind and just wants to talk to somebody quiet and nice. . . . I can tell when he's hungry or wants a beer before he even says anything. I know when his feet hurt him, I mean I *know* him and now I'm supposed to turn around and make a stranger out of him? I don't know why I have to do that, I mean.

RODOLPHO: Catherine. If I take in my hands a little bird. And she grows and wishes to fly. But I will not let her out of my hands because I love her so much, is that right for me to do? I don't say you must hate him; but anyway you must go, mustn't you? Catherine?

CATHERINE: *(Softly.)* Hold me.

RODOLPHO: *(Clasping her to him.)* Oh, my little girl.

CATHERINE: Teach me. *(She is weeping.)* I don't know anything, teach me, Rodolpho, hold me.
RODOLPHO: There's nobody here now. Come inside. Come. *(He is leading her toward the bedrooms.)* And don't cry any more.

(Two Females)*

Stage Door

by Edna Ferber and George S. Kaufman

The Play

The play concerns a group of young girls who come to New York to study acting and find jobs. The place is the Footlights Club, where the hopes, dreams, and failures of sixteen actresses are dramatized in a series of scenes. The central plot has to deal with Terry Randall, who fights against discouragement and all odds to achieve her dream of a life in the theater.

The Scene

Terry comes home to announce to her roommate that her Broadway show has closed after four performances. Terry, ever the fighter, can only stay defeated for a short period of time. Terry resolves to never give up her dream. Kaye, in despair, confides that she has no talent and is giving up acting.

Special Note: For the working of this scene, the actress playing Kaye will take Jud's lines and Bernstein and Madeleine will be cut.

(TERRY *enters, a drooping figure. A glance at the two occupants of the room. Her back to door, she slowly closes it behind her and slumps against it.*)

KAYE: Hello!

JUD: Hello, Terry.

TERRY: Young lady, willing, talented, not very beautiful, finds herself at liberty. *(As she starts R.)* Will double in brass, will polish brass, will eat brass before very long. Hi, girls!

KAYE: Terry, what's the matter?

TERRY: We closed. Four performances and we closed.

KAYE: Terry, you didn't!

JUD: Tonight! But it's only Thursday!

TERRY: *(Sitting in chair R.)* Well, it seems you can close on Thursday just as well as Saturday — in fact, it's even better: it gives you two more days to be sunk in.

JUD: But it didn't get bad notices. What happened?

TERRY: We just got to the theatre tonight, and there it was on the call-board. "To the Members of the 'Blue Grotto' Company: You are hereby advised that the engagement of the 'Blue Grotto' will terminate after tonight's performance. Signed, Milton H. Schwepper, for Berger Productions, Incorporated."

KAYE: Terry, how ghastly!

JUD: Just like that, huh?

TERRY: Just like that. We stood there for a minute and read it. Then we sort of got together in the dressing rooms and talked about it in whispers, the way you do at a funeral. And then we all put on our make-up and gave the best damned performance we'd ever given.

JUD: Any other job in the world, if you get canned you can have a good cry in the washroom and go home. But show business! You take it on the chin and then paint up your face and out on the stage as gay as anything. "My dear Lady Barbara, what an enchanting place you have here! And what a quaint idea, giving us pig's knuckles for tea!"

TERRY: Yes, it was awfully jolly. I wouldn't have minded if Berger or somebody had come back stage and said, "Look, we're sorry to do this to you, and better luck next time." But nobody came around — not Berger, or the author, or the director or anybody. They can all run away at a time like that, but the actors have to stay and face it.

JUD: You'll get something else, Terry. You got swell notices in this one.

TERRY: Nobody remembers notices except the actors who get them.

KAYE: The movie scouts remember. What about your screen test?

JUD: Yes, how about that? Have you heard from it?

TERRY: *(Rises and up to bureau R.)* Oh, I'm not counting on that. They might take Jean. She's got that camera face. But they'll never burn up the Coast wires over me.

JUD: Jean can't act. You're ten times the actress that she is.

TERRY: *(Throwing herself across bed.)* Oh, how do you know who's an actress and who isn't! You're an actress if you're acting. Without a job and those lines to say, an actress is just an ordinary person, trying not to look as scared as she feels. What is there about it, anyhow? Why do we all keep trying?

-------------------------------- CUT --------------------------------

BERN: *(Enters with mourning veil hat, followed by* MADELEINE *who has a dish in her hand.)* How do I look?
KAYE: Marvelous.
JUD: What are you?
BERN: I'm seeing the Theatre Guild tomorrow. They're going to revive "Madame X." *(Exit.)*
MAD: Anybody want some chop suey? Terry? Kaye?
TERRY: No, thank you.
KAYE: No, thanks.
JUD: *(Tempted by this.)* Chop suey? I thought it was rarebit.
MAD: We didn't have any beer, so I'm calling it chop suey. *(She goes.)*
JUD: Certainly sounds terrible. *(Crossing L. to door — turns with a hand on door.)* Look, I guess you want this closed, huh?
TERRY: Yes, please.
  (Door closes. KAYE *and* TERRY *are alone. With a sigh* TERRY *again faces reality. Listlessly she begins to undress.* KAYE *is almost ready for bed. As she turns back bedclothes she pauses to regard* TERRY.*)*

KAYE: I know how sunk you feel, Terry. It's that horrible letdown after the shock has worn off.
TERRY: The idiotic part of it is that I didn't feel so terrible after the first minute. I thought, well, Keith's coming around after the show, and we'll go to Smitty's and sit there and talk and it won't seem so bad. But he never showed up.
KAYE: Terry, I shouldn't try to advise you where men are concerned. I haven't been very smart myself — but this isn't the first time he's let you down. Don't get in too deep with a boy like Keith Burgess. It'll only make you unhappy.
TERRY: I don't expect him to be like other people. I wouldn't want him to be. One of the things that makes him so much fun is that he's different. If he forgets an appointment it's because he's working and doesn't notice. Only I wish he had come tonight. *(She is pulling her*

dress over her head as she talks and her words are partly muffled until she emerges.) I needed him so. *(Suddenly her defenses are down.)* Kaye, I'm frightened. For the first time, I'm frightened. It's three years now. The first year it didn't matter so much. I was so young. Nobody was ever as young as I was. I thought, they just don't know. But I'll get a good start and show them. I didn't mind anything in those days. Not having any money, or quite enough food; and a pair of silk stockings always a major investment. I didn't mind because I felt so sure that that wonderful part was going to come along. But it hasn't. And suppose it doesn't next year? Suppose it never comes?

KAYE: You can always go home. You've got a home to go to, anyhow.

TERRY: *(Rises.)* And marry some home-town boy — like Louise?

KAYE: I didn't mean that, exactly.

TERRY: I can't just go home and plump myself down on Dad. You know what a country doctor makes! When I was little I never knew how poor we were, because mother made everything seem so glamorous — so much fun. *(Starts L. for bathroom — all this time TERRY has continued her preparations for bed: hung up her dress, slipped her nightgown over her head.)* Even if I was sick it was a lot of fun, because then I was allowed to look at her scrap-book. I even used to pretend to be sick, just to look at it — and that took acting, with a doctor for a father. *(Exits and makes rest of change off stage continuing dialogue.)* I adored that scrap-book. All those rep-company actors in wooden attitudes — I remember a wonderful picture of mother as Esmeralda. It was the last part she ever played, and she never finished the performance.

KAYE: What happened?

TERRY: She fainted, right in the middle of the last act. They rang down and somebody said, "Is there a doctor in the house?" And there was. And he married her.

KAYE: Terry, how romantic!

TERRY: Only first she was sick for weeks and weeks. Of course the company had to leave her behind. They thought she'd catch up with them any week, but she never did.

KAYE: Didn't she ever miss it? I mean afterward.

TERRY: *(Coming back into room, crosses R. to bureau.)* I know now that she missed it every minute of her life. I think if Dad hadn't been such a gentle darling, and not so dependent on her, she might have gone off and taken me with her. I'd have been one of those children brought up in dressing rooms, sleeping in trunk trays, getting my vocabulary from stage-hands. *(As she creams her face.)*

KAYE: That would have been thrilling.

TERRY: But she didn't. She lived out the rest of her life right in that little town, but she was stage-struck to the end. There never was any doubt in her mind — I was going to be an actress. It was almost a spiritual thing, like being dedicated to the church.

KAYE: I never thought of the theatre that way. I just used it as a convenience, because I was desperate, and now I'm using it again because I'm desperate.

TERRY: Oh, now I've made you blue. I didn't mean to be gloomy. We're fine! We're elegant! They have to pay me two weeks' salary for this flop. Eighty dollars. We're fixed for two weeks. One of us'll get a job.

KAYE: I can't take any more money from you. You paid my twelve-fifty last week.

TERRY: Oh, don't be stuffy! I happened to be the one who was working.

KAYE: I'll never get a job. I'm — I'm not a very good actress.

TERRY: Oh, now!

KAYE: And there's nothing else I can do and nobody I can go back to. Except somebody I'll *never* go back to.

TERRY: It's your husband, isn't it?

KAYE: *(Looks at TERRY a moment, silently.)* I ran away from him twice before, but I had to go back. I was hungry, and finally I didn't even have a room. Both times, he just waited. He's waiting now.

TERRY: Kaye, tell me what is it? Why are you afraid of him?

KAYE: *(Turns her eyes away from TERRY as she speaks.)* Because I know him. To most people he's a normal attractive man. But I know better. Nights of terror. "Now, darling, it wouldn't do any good to kill me. They wouldn't let you play polo tomorrow. Now, we'll open the window and you'll throw the revolver at that lamp-post. It'll be such fun to hear the glass smash." And then there were the times when he made love to me. I can't even tell you about that. *(She recalls the scene with a shudder.)*

TERRY: Kaye, darling! But if he's as horrible as that, can't you do something legally?

KAYE: *(A desperate shake of her head.)* They have millions. I'm nobody. I've gone to his family. They're united like a stone wall. They treated me as though I was the mad one.

TERRY: But, Kaye, isn't there anybody — What about your own folks? Haven't you got any?

KAYE: I have a father. Chicago. I ran away at sixteen and went on the stage. Then I met Dick — and I fell for him. He was good-looking, and gay, and always doing sort of crazy things — smashing automobiles and shooting at bar-room mirrors . . . I thought it was funny, *then.*

TERRY: And I've been moaning about my little troubles.

KAYE: You know, I'd sworn to myself I never was going to bother you with this. Now, what made me do it!

TERRY: I'm glad you did. It'll do you good.

KAYE: Yes, I suppose it will.

TERRY: *(As she takes counterpane off bed.)* Well, we might as well get those sheep over the fence. Maybe we'll wake up tomorrow morning and there'll be nineteen managers downstairs, all saying, "You and only you can play this part."

KAYE: I suppose Jean'll be out till all hours.

TERRY: *(At window, puts up shade — electric sign comes on one-quarter up.) There's* a girl who hasn't got any troubles. Life rolls right along for her. . . . *(Puts up window.)* Well, ready to go bye-bye?

KAYE: *(Switches off all lights except bed lamps — electric sign up to one-half.)* I suppose I might as well. But I feel so wide awake.

Part 3: LANGUAGE AND STYLE
SCENES

Antigone

by Jean Anouilh
adapted by Lewis Galantiere

The Play

Jean Anouilh's modern dress retelling of Sophocles' *Antigone*. The updated Greek legend comes from a Paris that suffered under the tyranny of the Nazi occupation during World War II. The parallels between Hitler's rule and Creon's Thebes are evident. Creon has ordered that Eteocles shall be buried with honors while the corpse of Polynices is to be left to be mangled by the vultures and the dogs. Anyone who attempts to give Polynices burial is to be put to death. Antigone, a sister, defies the edict, heaps earth upon the dishonored corpse and is buried alive for punishment. This act brings about the suicide of Creon's son, Haemon, Antigone's betrothed.

The Scene

Antigone sends for Haemon so that she can apologize for a quarrel they had the night before. Haemon does not know that Antigone has defied Creon's edict and buried her brother, Polynices. Antigone professes her love for Haemon and then breaks off the relationship.

ANTIGONE: Haemon, Haemon! Forgive me for quarreling with you last night. *(She crosses quickly to Left* of HAEMON.*)* Forgive me for everything. It was all my fault. *(*HAEMON *moves a few steps toward her. They embrace.)* Oh, I beg you to forgive me.

HAEMON: You know that I've forgiven you. You had hardly slammed the door; your perfume still hung in the room, when I had already forgiven you. *(He holds her in his arms and smiles at her.)* You stole that perfume. From whom?

ANTIGONE: Ismene.

HAEMON: And the rouge, and the face powder, and the dress?

ANTIGONE: Ismene.

HAEMON: And in whose honor did you get yourself up so glamorously?

ANTIGONE: I'll tell you. *(She draws him closer.)* Oh, what a fool I was! To waste a whole evening! A whole, beautiful evening!

HAEMON: We'll have other evenings, my sweet.

ANTIGONE: Perhaps we won't.

HAEMON: And other quarrels, too. A happy love is full of quarrels.

ANTIGONE: A happy love, yes. Haemon, listen to me.

HAEMON: Yes?

ANTIGONE: And don't laugh at me this morning. Be serious.

HAEMON: I am serious.

ANTIGONE: And hold me tight. *Tighter* than you have ever held me. I want all your strength to flow into me.
(They embrace closer. His cheek against her upstage cheek.)

HAEMON: *There!* With all my strength.
(A pause.)

ANTIGONE: *(Breathless.)* That's good. *(They stand for a moment, silent and motionless.)* Haemon! I wanted to tell you. You know — The little boy we were going to have when we were married?

HAEMON: Yes?

ANTIGONE: I'd have protected him against everything in the world.

HAEMON: Yes, dear sweet.

ANTIGONE: Oh, you don't know how I should have held him in my arms and given him my strength. He wouldn't have been afraid of anything, Haemon. His mother wouldn't have been very imposing: her hair wouldn't have been very well brushed; but she would have been strong where he was concerned, so much stronger than any other mother in the world. You believe that, don't you, Haemon?

HAEMON: Yes, my dearest.

ANTIGONE: And you believe me when I say that *you* would have had a real wife?

HAEMON: *(Draws her into his arms.)* I *have* a real wife.

ANTIGONE: *(Pressing against him and crying out.)* Haemon, you loved me! You *did* love me that night. You're sure of it!

HAEMON: What night, my sweet?

ANTIGONE: And you are sure that that night, at the dance, when you came to the corner where I was sitting, there was no mistake? It was *me* you were looking for? It wasn't another girl? And that not in your secret heart of hearts, have you said to yourself that it was Ismene you ought to have asked to marry you?

HAEMON: *(Reproachfully.)* Antigone, you are idiotic. *(He kisses her.)*

ANTIGONE: Oh, you do love me, don't you? You love me as a woman — as a woman wants to be loved, don't you? Your arms around me aren't lying, are they? Your hands, so warm against my back — they aren't lies? This warmth; this strength that flows through me as I stand so close to you. They aren't lies, are they?

HAEMON: Antigone, my darling — I love you. *(He kisses her again.)*

ANTIGONE: *(Turns her head partly away from him.)* I'm sallow — and I'm not pretty. Ismene is pink and golden. She's like a fruit.

HAEMON: Antigone — !

ANTIGONE: Oh, forgive me, I am ashamed of myself. But this morning, this special morning, I must know. Tell me the truth! I beg you to tell me the truth! When you think of me, when it strikes you suddenly that I am going to belong to you — *(She looks at him)* do you get the sense that — that a great *empty* space — is being hollowed out inside you; and that there is something inside you that is just — dying?

HAEMON: Yes, I do.

(A pause as they face against one another.)

ANTIGONE: That's the way I feel. *(She clings to him for a moment.)* There! And now I have two things more to tell you. And when I have told them to you, you must go away instantly, without asking any questions. However strange they may seem to you. However much they may hurt you. Swear that you will!

(A pause, as HAEMON kisses her hand.)

HAEMON: *(Beginning to be troubled.)* What are these things that you are going to tell me?

ANTIGONE: Swear, first, that you will go away without a single word. Without so much as looking at me. *(She looks at him, wretched-*

ness in her face.) You hear me, Haemon. Swear, please. It's the
last *mad* wish that you will ever have to grant me.
(A pause.)

HAEMON: I swear it.

ANTIGONE: Thank you. Well, here it is. First, about last night, when I
went to your house. You asked me a moment ago *why* I wore
Ismene's dress and rouge. I did it because I was stupid. I wasn't
sure that you loved me — as a woman; and I did it because I
wanted you to want me.

HAEMON: Was *that* the reason? Oh, my poor —

ANTIGONE: *(Places her hand on his face.)* No! Wait! That was the
reason. And you laughed at me, and we quarreled, and I flung out
of the house. The reason why I went to your house last night was
that I wanted you to take me. I wanted to be your wife — before.

HAEMON: *(Questioningly.)* Antigone — ?

ANTIGONE: *(Shuts him off; Places both hands on his face.)* Haemon!
You swore you wouldn't ask a single question. You swore it,
Haemon. As a matter of fact, I'll tell you why. I wanted to be your
wife last night because I love you that way very — very strongly.
And also — because — Oh, my beloved — *(She removes her
hands from his face.)* I'm going to cause you such a lot of pain. I
wanted it also because *(She draws a step away from him.)* I shall
never — never be able to marry you, never!

HAEMON: *(Moves a step toward her.)* Antigone — !

ANTIGONE: *(She moves a few steps away from him.)* Haemon! You
took a solemn oath! You swore! Leave me now! Tomorrow the
whole thing will be clear to you. Even before tomorrow: this afternoon. *(He makes a slight gesture toward her.)* If you *please,*
Haemon, go now. It's the only thing left that you can do for me if
you still love me. *(A pause as HAEMON stares at her. Then he
turns and goes out through the arch Right. ANTIGONE stands
motionless. In a strange, gentle voice, as of calm after the storm,
she speaks:)* Well, it's over for Haemon, Antigone.

Arcadia

by Tom Stoppard

The Play

This play moves back and forth between 1809 and the present at the elegant estate owned by the Coverly family. The 1809 scenes reveal a household in transition. As the Arcadian landscape is being transformed into picturesque Gothic gardens, complete with a hermitage, Lady Thomasina and her tutor delve into intellectual and romantic issues. Present-day scenes depict the Coverly descendants and two competing scholars who are researching a present-day scandal at the estate involving Lord Byron.

The Scene

Thomasina is taking a lesson in mathematics from her tutor, Septimus. However, Thomasina has questions about a very different subject.

THOMASINA: Septimus, what is carnal embrace?
SEPTIMUS: Carnal embrace is the practice of throwing one's arms around a side of beef.
THOMASINA: Is that all?
SEPTIMUS: No . . . a shoulder of mutton, a haunch of venison well hugged, an embrace of grouse . . . *caro, carnis:* feminine; flesh.
THOMASINA: Is it a sin?

SEPTIMUS: Not necessarily, my lady, but when carnal embrace is sinful it is a sin of the flesh, QED. We had *caro* in our Gallic Wars — "The Britons live on milk and meat" — *"lacte et came vivunt."* I am sorry that the seed fell on stony ground.

THOMASINA: That was the sin of Onan, wasn't it, Septimus?

SEPTIMUS: Yes. He was giving his brother's wife a Latin lesson and she was hardly the wiser after it than before. I thought you were finding a proof for Fermat's last theorem.

THOMASINA: It is very difficult, Septimus. You will have to show me how.

SEPTIMUS: If I knew how, there would be no need to ask *you.* Fermat's last theorem has kept people busy for a hundred and fifty years, and I hoped it would keep *you* busy long enough for me to read Mr. Chater's poem in praise of love with only the distraction of its own absurdities.

THOMASINA: Our Mr. Chater has written a poem?

SEPTIMUS: He believes he has written a poem, yes. I can see that there might be more carnality in your algebra than in Mr. Chater's "Couch of Eros."

THOMASINA: Oh, it was not my algebra. I heard Jellaby telling cook that Mrs. Chater was discovered in carnal embrace in the gazebo.

SEPTIMUS: *(Pause.)* Really? With whom, did Jellaby happen to say? *(THOMASINA considers this with a puzzled frown.)*

THOMASINA: What do you mean, with whom?

SEPTIMUS: With what? Exactly so. The idea is absurd. Where did this story come from?

THOMASINA: Mr. Noakes.

SEPTIMUS: Mr. Noakes!

THOMASINA: Papa's landskip architect. He was taking bearings in the garden when he saw — through his spyglass — Mrs. Chater in the gazebo in carnal embrace.

SEPTIMUS: And do you mean to tell me that Mr. Noakes told the butler?

THOMASINA: No. Mr. Noakes told Mr. Chater. Jellaby was told by the groom, who overheard Mr. Noakes telling Mr. Chater, in the stable yard.

SEPTIMUS: Mr. Chater being engaged in closing the stable door.

THOMASINA: What do you mean, Septimus?

SEPTIMUS: So, thus far, the only people who know about this are Mr. Noakes the landskip architect, the groom, the butler, the cook and, of course, Mrs. Chater's husband, the poet.

THOMASINA: And Arthur who was cleaning the silver, and the boot-boy. And now you.

SEPTIMUS: Of course. What else did he say?

THOMASINA: Mr. Noakes?

SEPTIMUS: No, not Mr. Noakes. Jellaby. You heard Jellaby telling the cook.

THOMASINA: Cook hushed him almost as soon as he started. Jellaby did not see that I was being allowed to finish yesterday's upstairs' rabbit pie before I came to my lesson. I think you have not been candid with me, Septimus. A gazebo is not, after all, a meat larder.

SEPTIMUS: I never said my definition was complete.

THOMASINA: Is carnal embrace kissing?

SEPTIMUS: Yes.

THOMASINA: And throwing one's arms around Mrs. Chater?

SEPTIMUS: Yes. Now, Fermat's last theorem —

THOMASINA: I thought as much. I hope you are ashamed.

SEPTIMUS: I, my lady?

THOMASINA: If *you* do not teach me the true meaning of things, who will?

SEPTIMUS: Ah. Yes, I am ashamed. Carnal embrace is sexual congress, which is the insertion of the male genital organ into the female genital organ for purposes of procreation and pleasure. Fermat's last theorem, by contrast, asserts that when x, y and z are whole numbers each raised to power of n, the sum of the first two can never equal the third when n is greater than 2.
(Pause.)

THOMASINA: Eurghhh!

SEPTIMUS: Nevertheless, that is the theorem.

THOMASINA: It is disgusting and incomprehensible. Now when I am grown to practise it myself I shall never do so without thinking of you.

SEPTIMUS: Thank you very much, my lady. Was Mrs. Chater down this morning?

THOMASINA: No. Tell me more about sexual congress.

SEPTIMUS: There is nothing more to be said about sexual congress.

THOMASINA: Is it the same as love?

SEPTIMUS: Oh no, it is much nicer than that.
(One of the side doors leads to the music room. It is the other side door which now opens to admit JELLABY, *the butler.)*

SEPTIMUS: I am teaching, Jellaby.

JELLABY: Beg your pardon, Mr. Hodge, Mr. Chater said it was urgent you receive his letter.

SEPTIMUS: Oh, very well. *(SEPTIMUS takes the letter.)* Thank you. *(And to dismiss* JELLABY.*)* Thank you.

JELLABY: *(Holding his ground.)* Mr. Chater asked me to bring him your answer.

SEPTIMUS: My answer? *(He opens the letter. There is no envelope as such, but there is a 'cover' which, folded and sealed, does the same service.* SEPTIMUS *tosses the cover negligently aside and reads.)* Well, my answer is that as is my custom and my duty to his lordship I am engaged until a quarter to twelve in the education of his daughter. When I am done, and if Mr. Chater is still there, I will be happy to wait upon him in — *(He checks the letter.)* — in the gunroom.

JELLABY: I will tell him so, thank you, sir.

(SEPTIMUS folds the letter and places it between the pages of "The Couch of Eros.")

THOMASINA: What is for dinner, Jellaby?

JELLABY: Boiled ham and cabbages, my lady, and a rice pudding.

THOMASINA: Oh, goody.

(JELLABY leaves.)

SEPTIMUS: Well, so much for Mr. Noakes. He puts himself forward as a gentleman, a philosopher of the picturesque, a visionary who can move mountains and cause lakes, but in the scheme of the garden he is as the serpent.

THOMASINA: When you stir your rice pudding, Septimus, the spoonful of jam spreads itself round making red trails like the picture of a meteor in my astronomical atlas. But if you stir backward, the jam will not come together again. Indeed, the pudding does not notice and continues to turn pink just as before. Do you think this is odd?

SEPTIMUS: No.

THOMASINA: Well, I do. You cannot stir things apart.

SEPTIMUS: No more you can, time must needs run backward, and since it will not, we must stir our way onward mixing as we go, disorder out of disorder into disorder until pink is complete, unchanging and unchangeable, and we are done with it forever. This is known as free will or self-determination. *(He picks up the tortoise and moves it a few inches as though it had strayed, on top of some loose papers, and admonishes it.)* Sit!

THOMASINA: Septimus, do you think God is a Newtonian?

SEPTIMUS: An Etonian? Almost certainly, I'm afraid. We must ask
your brother to make it his first inquiry.

THOMASINA: No, Septimus, a Newtonian. Septimus! Am I the first
person to have thought of this?

SEPTIMUS: No.

THOMASINA: I have not said yet.

SEPTIMUS: "If everything from the furthest planet to the smallest
atom of our brain acts according to Newton's law of motion, what
becomes of free will?"

THOMASINA: No.

SEPTIMUS: God's will.

THOMASINA: No.

SEPTIMUS: Sin.

THOMASINA: *(Derisively.)* No!

SEPTIMUS: Very well.

THOMASINA: If you could stop every atom in its position and direction, and if your mind could comprehend all the actions thus sus-
pended, then if you were really, *really* good at algebra you could
write the formula for all the future; and although nobody can be
so clever to do it, the formula must exist just as if one could.

SEPTIMUS: *(Pause.)* Yes. *(Pause.)* Yes, as far as I know, you are the
first person to have thought of this. *(Pause. With an effort.)* In the
margin of his copy of *Arithmetica*, Fermat wrote that he had discovered a wonderful proof of his theorem but, the margin being
too narrow for his purpose, did not have room to write it down.
The note was found after his death, and from that day to this —

THOMASINA: Oh! I see now! The answer is perfectly obvious.

SEPTIMUS: This time you may have overreached yourself.

(One Female and One Male)

The Importance of Being Earnest
by Oscar Wilde

The Play

A witty and satirical comedy of manners revolving around an ingenious case of manufactured mistaken identity. Two young Victorian gentlemen, Jack and Algernon, seek the hands of two young ladies, Cecily and Gwendolen. Cecily loves Algernon, while Gwendolen loves Jack. However, each has said they could only love a man with the first name of Ernest. The obstacles facing these two young men are no more serious than the young men themselves. Oscar Wilde said of the play: "It is exquisitely trivial, a delicate bubble of froth, and it has as its philosophy . . . that we should treat all the trivial things of life seriously and all the serious things of life with sincere and studied triviality."

The Scene

Algernon has just confided to the audience that he is in love with Cecily, who, under the guise of coming back to water the roses, is discovered by Algernon. Algy declares his love and asks for her hand in marriage. Cecily (thinking that his name is Ernest) accepts. Cecily then confides to her beloved that she could only marry a man named Ernest. Algernon plans a hasty baptism to solve this problem.

(Enter CECILY *at the back of the garden. She picks up the can and begins to water the flowers.)*

ALGERNON: But I must see her before I go, and make arrangements for another Bunbury. Ah, there she is.

CECILY: Oh, I merely came back to water the roses. I thought you were with Uncle Jack.

ALGERNON: He's gone to order the dog-cart for me.

CECILY: Oh, is he going to take you for a nice drive?

ALGERNON: He's going to send me away.

CECILY: Then have we got to part?

ALGERNON: I am afraid so. It's a very painful parting.

CECILY: It is always painful to part from people whom one has known for a very brief space of time. The absence of old friends one can endure with equanimity. But even a momentary separation from anyone to whom one has just been introduced is almost unbearable.

ALGERNON: Thank you.
(Enter MERRIMAN.)

MERRIMAN: The dog-cart is at the door, sir. (ALGERNON *looks appealingly at* CECILY.)

CECILY: It can wait, Merriman . . . for . . . five minutes.

MERRIMAN: Yes, Miss. *(Exit MERRIMAN.)*

ALGERNON: I hope, Cecily, I shall not offend you if I state quite frankly and openly that you seem to me to be in every way the visible personification of absolute perfection.

CECILY: I think your frankness does you great credit, Ernest. If you will allow me I will copy your remarks into my diary. *(Goes over to table and begins writing in diary.)*

ALGERNON: Do you really keep a diary? I'd give anything to look at it. May I?

CECILY: Oh, no. *(Puts her hand over it.)* You see, it is simply a very young girl's record of her own thoughts and impressions, and consequently meant for publication. When it appears in volume form I hope you will order a copy. But pray, Ernest, don't stop. I delight in taking down from dictation. I have reached "absolute perfection." You can go on. I am quite ready for more.

ALGERNON: *(Somewhat taken aback.)* Ahem! Ahem!

CECILY: Oh, don't cough, Ernest. When one is dictating one should speak fluently and not cough. Besides, I don't know how to spell a cough. *(Writes as ALGERNON speaks.)*

ALGERNON: *(Speaking very rapidly.)* Cecily, ever since I first looked upon your wonderful and incomparable beauty, I have dared to love you wildly, passionately, devotedly, hopelessly.

CECILY: I don't think that you should tell me that you love me wildly, passionately, devotedly, hopelessly. Hopelessly doesn't seem to make much sense, does it?

ALGERNON: Cecily!

(Enter MERRIMAN.*)*

MERRIMAN: The dog-cart is waiting, sir.

ALGERNON: Tell it to come round next week, at the same hour.

MERRIMAN: *(Looks at* CECILY, *who makes no sign.)* Yes, sir. *(He retires.)*

CECILY: Uncle Jack would be very annoyed if he knew you were staying on till next week, at the same hour.

ALGERNON: Oh, I don't care about Jack. I do not care for anybody in the whole world but you. I love you, Cecily. You will marry me, won't you?

CECILY: You silly boy! Of course. Why, we have been engaged for the last three months.

ALGERNON: For the last three months?

CECILY: Yes, it will be exactly three months on Thursday.

ALGERNON: But how did we become engaged?

CECILY: Well, ever since dear Uncle Jack first confessed to us that he had a younger brother who was very wicked and bad, you of course have formed the chief topic of conversation between myself and Miss Prism. And of course a man who is much talked about is always very attractive. One feels there must be something in him after all. I daresay it was foolish of me, but I fell in love with you, Ernest.

ALGERNON: Darling! And when was the engagement actually settled?

CECILY: On the 14th of February last. Worn out by your entire ignorance of my existence, I determined to end the matter one way or the other, and after a long struggle with myself I accepted you under this dear old tree here. The next day I bought this little ring in your name, and this is the little bangle with the true lovers' knot I promised you always to wear.

ALGERNON: Did I give you this? It's very pretty, isn't it?

CECILY: Yes, you've wonderfully good taste, Ernest. It's the excuse I've always given for your leading such a bad life. And this is the box in which I keep all your dear letters. *(Kneels at table, opens box, and produces letters tied up with blue ribbon.)*

ALGERNON: My letters! But my own sweet Cecily, I have never written you any letters.

CECILY: You need hardly remind me of that, Ernest. I remember only too well that I was forced to write your letters for you. I wrote always three times a week, and sometimes oftener.

ALGERNON: Oh, do let me read them, Cecily?

CECILY: Oh! I couldn't possibly. They would make you far too conceited. *(Replaces box.)* The three you wrote me after I had broken off the engagement are so beautiful, and so badly spelled, that even now I can hardly read them without crying a little.

ALGERNON: But was our engagement ever broken off?

CECILY: Of course it was. On the 22nd of last March. You can see the entry if you like. *(Shows diary.)* "Today I broke off my engagement with Ernest. I feel it is better to do so. The weather still continues charming."

ALGERNON: But why on earth did you break it off? What had I done? I had done nothing at all. Cecily, I am very much hurt indeed to hear you broke it off. Particularly when the weather was so charming.

CECILY: It would hardly have been a really serious engagement if it hadn't been broken off at least once. But I forgave you before the week was out.

ALGERNON: *(Crossing to her and kneeling.)* What a perfect angel you are, Cecily.

CECILY: You dear romantic boy. *(He kisses her, she puts her fingers through his hair.)* I hope your hair curls naturally, does it?

ALGERNON: Yes, darling, with a little help from others.

CECILY: I am so glad.

ALGERNON: You'll never break off our engagement again, Cecily?

CECILY: I don't think I could break it off now that I have actually met you. Besides, of course, there is the question of your name.

ALGERNON: Yes, of course. *(Nervously.)*

CECILY: You must not laugh at me, darling, but it had always been a girlish dream of mine to love someone whose name was Ernest. *(*ALGERNON *rises,* CECILY *also.)* There is something in that name that seems to inspire absolute confidence. I pity any poor married woman whose husband is not called Ernest.

ALGERNON: But, my dear child, do you mean to say you could not love me if I had some other name?

CECILY: But what name?

ALGERNON: Oh, any name you like — Algernon — for instance . . .

CECILY: But I don't like the name of Algernon.

ALGERNON: Well, my own dear, sweet, loving little darling, I really can't see why you should object to the name of Algernon. It is not at all a bad name. In fact, it is rather an aristocratic name. Half of the chaps who get into the Bankruptcy Court are called Algernon. But seriously, Cecily. . . *(Moving to her.)* . . . if my name was Algy, couldn't you love me?

CECILY: *(Rising.)* I might respect you, Ernest, I might admire your character, but I fear that I should not be able to give you my undivided attention.

ALGERNON: Ahem! Cecily! *(Picking up hat.)* Your Rector here is, I suppose, thoroughly experienced in the practice of all the rites and ceremonials of the Church?

CECILY: Oh, yes. Dr. Chasuble is a most learned man. He has never written a single book, so you can imagine how much he knows.

ALGERNON: I must see him at once on a most important christening — I mean on most important business.

CECILY: Oh!

ALGERNON: I shan't be away more than half an hour.

CECILY: Considering that we have been engaged since February the 14th, and that I only met you today for the first time, I think it is rather hard that you should leave me for so long a period as half an hour. Couldn't you make it twenty minutes?

ALGERNON: I'll be back in no time. *(Kisses her and rushes down the garden.)*

CECILY: What an impetuous boy he is! I like his hair so much. I must enter his proposal in my diary.

* * * * *

The Scene

Jack, taking advantage of Lady Bracknell's temporary absence, declares his love for Gwendolen. Gwendolen (thinking that his name is Ernest), declares her love. She then confides to her beloved that she could only marry a man named Ernest. Jack, after unsuccessfully trying to dissuade Gwendolen on the merits of the name Ernest, asks for her hand in marriage. He is discovered on his knees by the formidable Lady Bracknell.

JACK: Charming day it has been, Miss Fairfax.

GWENDOLEN: Pray don't talk to me about the weather, Mr. Worthing. Whenever people talk to me about the weather, I always feel quite certain that they mean something else. And that makes me so nervous.

JACK: I do mean something else.

GWENDOLEN: I thought so. In fact, I am never wrong.

JACK: And I would like to be allowed to take advantage of Lady Bracknell's temporary absence . . .

GWENDOLEN: I would certainly advise you to do so. Mamma has a way of coming back suddenly into a room that I have often had to speak to her about.

JACK: *(Nervously.)* Miss Fairfax, ever since I met you I have admired you more than any girl . . . I have ever met since . . . I met you.

GWENDOLEN: Yes, I am quite aware of the fact. And I often wish that in public, at any rate, you had been more demonstrative. For me you have always had an irresistible fascination. Even before I met you I was far from indifferent to you. *(JACK looks at her in amazement.)* We live, as I hope you know, Mr. Worthing, in an age of ideals. The fact is constantly mentioned in the more expensive monthly magazines, and has reached the provincial pulpits I am told; and my ideal has always been to love someone of the name of Ernest. There is something in that name that inspires absolute confidence. The moment Algernon first mentioned to me that he had a friend called Ernest, I knew I was destined to love you.

JACK: You really love me, Gwendolen?

GWENDOLEN: Passionately!

JACK: Darling! You don't know how happy you've made me.

GWENDOLEN: My own Ernest!

JACK: But you don't really mean to say that you couldn't love me if my name wasn't Ernest?

GWENDOLEN: But your name is Ernest.

JACK: Yes, I know it is. But supposing it was something else? Do you mean to say you couldn't love me then?

GWENDOLEN: *(Glibbly.)* Ah! that is clearly a metaphysical speculation, and like most metaphysical speculations has very little reference at all to the actual facts of real life, as we know them.

JACK: Personally, darling, to speak quite candidly, I don't much care about the name of Ernest . . . I don't think the name suits me at all.

GWENDOLEN: It suits you perfectly. It is a divine name. It has a music of its own. It produces vibrations.

JACK: Well, really, Gwendolen, I must say that I think there are lots of other much nicer names. I think Jack, for instance, a charming name.

GWENDOLEN: Jack? . . . No, there is very little music in the name Jack, if any at all, indeed. It does not thrill. It produces absolutely no vibrations . . . I have known several Jacks, and they all, without exception, were more than usually plain. Besides, Jack is a notorious domesticity for John! And I pity any woman who is married to a man called John. She would probably never be allowed to know the entrancing pleasure of a single moment's solitude. The only really safe name is Ernest.

JACK: Gwendolen, I must get christened at once — I mean we must get married at once. There is no time to be lost.

GWENDOLEN: Married, Mr. Worthing?

JACK: *(Astounded.)* Well . . . surely. You know that I love you, and you led me to believe, Miss Fairfax, that you were not absolutely indifferent to me.

GWENDOLEN: I adore you. But you haven't proposed to me yet. Nothing has been said at all about marriage. The subject has not even been touched on.

JACK: Well . . . may I propose to you now?

GWENDOLEN: I think it would be an admirable opportunity. And to spare you any possible disappointment, Mr. Worthing, I think it only fair to tell you quite frankly beforehand that I am fully determined to accept you.

JACK: Gwendolen!

GWENDOLEN: Yes, Mr. Worthing, what have you got to say to me?

JACK: You know what I have got to say to you.

GWENDOLEN: Yes, but you don't say it.

JACK: Gwendolen, will you marry me? *(Goes on his knees.)*

GWENDOLEN: Of course I will, darling. How long you have been about it! I am afraid you have had very little experience in how to propose.

JACK: My own one, I have never loved any one in the world but you.

GWENDOLEN: Yes, but men often propose for practice. I know my brother Gerald does. All my girl-friends tell me so. What wonderfully blue eyes you have, Ernest! They are quite, quite blue. I hope you will always look at me just like that, especially when there are other people present.

Widowers' Houses

by George Bernard Shaw

The Play

The play tackles issues of greed, poverty, and social inequality in Victorian England. A young doctor, Harry Trench, discovers that the fortune of his fiancée, Blanche Sartorius, derives from her father's exploitation of the poor. But he is converted (in an unexpected way) to Sartorius's views. The author describes this as an exposé of "middle class respectability and younger son gentility feeding on the poverty of the slum as flies fatten on filth."

The Scene

After discovering the source of Blanche's fortune, Trench insists that they live solely on his yearly income of seven hundred pounds. Outraged, Blanche believes this incomprehensible idea is merely an excuse to break off their engagement.

> *They go out together, laughing at him. He collapses into a chair shuddering in every nerve.* BLANCHE *appears at the door. Her face lights up when she sees that he is alone. She trips noiselessly to the back of his chair and clasps her hands over his eyes. With a convulsive start and exclamation he springs up and breaks away from her.*

BLANCHE: *(Astonished.)* Harry!

TRENCH: *(With distracted politeness.)* I beg your pardon. I was thinking — wont you sit down?

BLANCHE: *(Looking suspiciously at him.)* Is anything the matter?
(She sits down slowly near the writing table. He takes COKANE*'s
chair.)*

TRENCH: No. Oh no.

BLANCHE: Papa has not been disagreeable, I hope.

TRENCH: No: I have hardly spoken to him since I was with you. *(He
rises; takes up his chair; and plants it beside hers. This pleases
her better. She looks at him with her most winning smile. A sort of
sob breaks from him; and he catches her hands and kisses them
passionately. Then, looking into her eyes with intense earnestness,
he says)* Blanche: are you fond of money?

BLANCHE: *(Gaily.)* Very. Are you going to give me any?

TRENCH: *(Wincing.)* Dont make a joke of it: I'm serious. Do you
know that we shall be very poor?

BLANCHE: Is that what made you look as if you had neuralgia?

TRENCH: *(Pleadingly.)* My dear: it's no laughing matter. Do you
know that I have a bare seven hundred a year to live on?

BLANCHE: How dreadful!

TRENCH: Blanche, it's very serious indeed: I assure you it is.

BLANCHE: It would keep me rather short in my housekeeping, dearest
boy, if I had nothing of my own. But papa has promised me that I
shall be richer than ever when we are married.

TRENCH: We must do the best we can with seven hundred. I think we
ought to be self-supporting.

BLANCHE: Thats just what I mean to be, Harry. If I were to eat up
half your seven hundred, I should be making you twice as poor;
but I'm going to make you twice as rich instead. *(He shakes his
head.)* Has papa made any difficulty?

TRENCH: *(Rising with a sigh and taking his chair back to its former
place.)* No. None at all. *(He sits down dejectedly. When
BLANCHE speaks again her face and voice betray the beginning
of a struggle with her temper.)*

BLANCHE: Harry, are you too proud to take money from my father?

TRENCH: Yes, Blanche: I am too proud.

BLANCHE: *(After a pause.)* That is not nice to me, Harry.

TRENCH: You must bear with me, Blanche. I — I cant explain. After
all, it's very natural.

BLANCHE: Has it occurred to you that I may be proud too?

TRENCH: Oh, thats nonsense. No one will — accuse you of marrying for money.

BLANCHE: No one would think the worse of me if I did, or of you either. *(She rises and begins to walk restlessly about.)* We really cannot live on seven hundred a year, Harry; and I dont think it quite fair of you to ask me merely because you are afraid of people talking.

TRENCH: It's not that alone, Blanche.

BLANCHE: What else is it, then?

TRENCH. Nothing. I —

BLANCHE: *(Getting behind him, and speaking with forced playfulness as she bends over him, her hands on his shoulders.)* Of course, it's nothing. Now dont be absurd, Harry, be good and listen to me: I know how to settle it. You are too proud to owe anything to me; and I am too proud to owe anything to you. You have seven hundred a year. Well, I will take just seven hundred a year from papa at first; and then we shall be quits. Now, now, Harry, you know you've not a word to say against that.

TRENCH: It's impossible.

BLANCHE: Impossible!

TRENCH: Yes, impossible. I have resolved not to take any money from your father.

BLANCHE: But he'll give the money to me, not to you.

TRENCH: It's the same thing. *(With an effort to be sentimental.)* I love you too well to see any distinction. *(He puts up his hand half-heartedly. She takes it over his shoulder with equal indecision. They are both trying hard to conciliate one another.)*

BLANCHE: Thats a very nice way of putting it, Harry; but I'm sure there's something I ought to know. Has papa been disagreeable?

TRENCH: No: he has been very kind — to me, at least. It's not that. It's nothing you can guess, Blanche. It would only pain you — perhaps offend you. I dont mean, of course, that we shall live always on seven hundred a year. I intend to go at my profession in earnest, and work my fingers to the bone.

BLANCHE: *(Playing with his fingers, still over his shoulder.)* But I shouldnt like you with your fingers worked to the bone, Harry. I must be told what the matter is. *(He takes his hand quickly away: she flushes angrily; and her voice is no longer even an imitation of the voice of a lady as she exclaims.)* I hate secrets; and I dont like to be treated as if I were a child.

TRENCH: *(Annoyed by her tone.)* Theres nothing to tell. I dont choose to trespass on your father's generosity: thats all.

BLANCHE: You had no objection half an hour ago, when you met me in the hall, and shewed me all the letters. Your family doesnt object. Do you object?

TRENCH: *(Earnestly.)* I do not indeed. It's only a question of money.

BLANCHE: *(Imploringly, the voice softening and refining for the last time.)* Harry: theres no use in our fencing in this way. Papa will never consent to my being absolutely dependent on you; and I dont like the idea of it myself. If you even mention such a thing to him you will break off the match: you will indeed.

TRENCH: *(Obstinately.)* I cant help that.

BLANCHE *(White with rage.)* You cant help — ! Oh, I'm beginning to understand. I will save you the trouble. You can tell papa that *I* have broken off the match; and then there will be no further difficulty.

TRENCH: *(Taken aback.)* What do you mean, Blanche? Are you offended?

BLANCHE: Offended! How dare you ask me?

TRENCH: Dare!

BLANCHE: How much more manly it would have been to confess that you were trifling with me that time on the Rhine! Why did you come here today? Why did you write to your people?

TRENCH: Well, Blanche, if you are going to lose your temper —

BLANCHE: Thats no answer. You depended on your family to get you out of your engagement; and they did not object: they were only too glad to be rid of you. You were not mean enough to stay away, and not manly enough to tell the truth. You thought you could provoke me to break the engagement: thats so like a man — to try to put the woman in the wrong. Well, you have your way: I release you. I wish youd opened my eyes by downright brutality; by striking me; by anything rather than shuffling as you have done.

TRENCH: *(Hotly.)* Shuffling! If I'd thought you capable of turning on me like this, I'd never have spoken to you. Ive a good mind never to speak to you again.

BLANCHE: You shall not — not ever. I will take care of that *(going to the door.)*

TRENCH: *(Alarmed.)* What are you going to do?

BLANCHE: To get your letters: your false letters, and your presents: your hateful presents, to return them to you. I'm very glad it's all broken off; and if —

You Never Can Tell

by George Bernard Shaw

The Play

A pleasant comedy about the battle of the sexes. The devil may care
Mr. Valentine is a dentist in the seaside resort of Devon, and not terri-
bly successful. He owes his curmudgeon of a landlord six weeks' rent.
Into his life drops Gloria, a young woman with a decidedly feminist
outlook, thanks to her mother, a formidable expert on everything twen-
tieth century. Quite smitten, Valentine pursues Gloria. Gloria rebuffs
and retreats. Valentine's curmudgeon landlord turns out to be Gloria's
estranged father, who has not seen her, her twin siblings, or her mother
in eighteen years. The family is helped through their confusion by a
wise, elderly waiter who always makes people concentrate on social
niceties at trying moments.

The Scene

Valentine, smitten with Gloria and armed with a game plan, tries to
seduce the feminist Gloria. Gloria discovers that intellectual prowess is
no protection against old-fashioned love and flees from the appealing
Mr. Valentine.

VALENTINE: *(Panting.)* Whats the matter? *(Looking round.)* Wheres
    Crampton?

GLORIA: Gone. *(Valentine's face lights up with sudden joy, dread, and mischief as he realizes that he is alone with* GLORIA. *She continues indifferently.)* I thought he was ill; but he recovered himself. He wouldnt wait for you. I am sorry. *(She goes for her book and parasol.)*

VALENTINE: So much the better. He gets on my nerves after a while. *(Pretending to forget himself.)* How could that man have so beautiful a daughter!

GLORIA: *(Taken aback for a moment; then answering him with polite but intentional contempt.)* That seems to be an attempt at what is called a pretty speech. Let me say at once, Mr Valentine, that pretty speeches make very sickly conversation. Pray let us be friends, if we are to be friends, in a sensible and wholesome way. I have no intention of getting married; and unless you are content to accept that state of things, we had much better not cultivate each other's acquaintance.

VALENTINE: *(Cautiously.)* I see. May I ask just this one question? Is your objection an objection to marriage as an institution, or merely an objection to marrying me personally?

GLORIA: I do not know you well enough, Mr Valentine, to have any opinion on the subject of your personal merits. *(She turns away from him with infinite indifference, and sits down with her book on the garden seat.)* I do not think the conditions of marriage at present are such as any self-respecting woman can accept.

VALENTINE: *(Instantly changing his tone for one of cordial sincerity, as if he frankly accepted her terms and was delighted and reassured by her principles.)* Oh, then thats a point of sympathy between us already. I quite agree with you: the conditions are most unfair. *(He takes off his hat and throws it gaily on the iron table.)* No: what I want is to get rid of all that nonsense. *(He sits down beside her, so naturally that she does not think of objecting, and proceeds, with enthusiasm.)* Dont you think it a horrible thing that a man and a woman can hardly know one another without being supposed to have designs of that kind? As if there were no other interests! no other subjects of conversation! As if women were capable of nothing better!

GLORIA: *(Interested.)* Ah, now you are beginning to talk humanly and sensibly, Mr Valentine.

VALENTINE: *(With a gleam in his eye at the success of his hunter's guile.)* Of course! two intelligent people like us! Isnt it pleasant, in this stupid convention-ridden world, to meet with someone on the same plane? someone with an unprejudiced enlightened mind?

GLORIA: *(Earnestly.)* I hope to meet many such people in England.

VALENTINE: *(Dubiously.)* Hm! there are a good many people here: nearly forty millions. Theyre not all consumptive members of the highly educated classes like the people in Madeira.

GLORIA: *(Now full of her subject.)* Oh, everybody is stupid and prejudiced in Madeira; weak sentimental creatures. I hate weakness; and I hate sentiment.

VALENTINE: Thats what makes you so inspiring.

GLORIA: *(With a slight laugh.)* Am I inspiring?

VALENTINE: Yes. Strength's infectious.

GLORIA: Weakness is, I know.

VALENTINE: *(With conviction.)* Youre strong. Do you know that you changed the world for me this morning? I was in the dumps, thinking of my unpaid rent, frightened about the future. When you came in, I was dazzled. *(Her brow clouds a little. He goes on quickly.)* That was silly, of course; but really and truly something happened to me. Explain it how you will, my blood got — *(He hesitates, trying to think of a sufficiently unimpassioned word.)* — oxygenated: my muscles braced; my mind cleared; my courage rose. Thats odd, isnt it? considering that I am not at all a sentimental man.

GLORIA: *(Uneasily, rising.)* Let us go back to the beach.

VALENTINE: *(Darkly: looking up at her.)* What! you feel it too?

GLORIA: Feel what?

VALENTINE: Dread.

GLORIA: Dread?

VALENTINE: As if something were going to happen. It came over me suddenly just before you proposed that we should run away to the others.

GLORIA: *(Amazed.)* Thats strange: very strange! I had the same presentiment.

VALENTINE: *(Solemnly.)* How extraordinary. *(Rising.)* Well: shall we run away?

GLORIA: Run away! Oh no: that would be childish. *(She sits down again. He resumes his seat beside her, and watches her with a gravely sympathetic air. She is thoughtful and a little troubled as she adds.)* I wonder what is the scientific explanation of those fancies that cross us occasionally!

VALENTINE: Ah, I wonder! It's a curiously helpless sensation: isnt it?

GLORIA: *(Rebelling against the word.)* Helpless?

VALENTINE: Yes, helpless. As if Nature, after letting us belong to ourselves and do what we judged right and reasonable for all these years, were suddenly lifting her great hand to take us — her two little children — by the scruffs of our little necks, and use us, in spite of ourselves, for her own purposes, in her own way.

GLORIA: Isnt that rather fanciful?

VALENTINE: *(With a new and startling transition to a tone of utter recklessness.)* I dont know. I dont care. *(Bursting out reproachfully.)* Oh, Miss Clandon, Miss Clandon: how could you?

GLORIA: What have I done?

VALENTINE: Thrown this enchantment on me. I'm honestly trying to be sensible and scientific and everything that you wish me to be. But — but — oh, dont you see what you have set to work in my imagination?

GLORIA: I hope you are not going to be so foolish — so vulgar — as to say love.

VALENTINE: No, no, no, no. Not love: we know better than that. Let's call it chemistry. You cant deny that there is such a thing as chemical action, chemical affinity, chemical combination: the most irresistible of all natural forces. Well, youre attracting me irresistibly. Chemically.

GLORIA: *(Contemptuously.)* Nonsense!

VALENTINE: Of course it's nonsense, you stupid girl. *(Gloria recoils in outraged surprise.)* Yes, stupid girl: thats a scientific fact, anyhow. Youre a prig: a feminine prig: thats what you are. *(Rising)* Now I suppose youve done with me for ever. *(He goes to the iron table and takes up his hat.)*

GLORIA: *(With elaborate calm, sitting up like a High-school-mistress posing to be photographed.)* That shews how very little you understand my real character. I am not in the least offended. *(He pauses and puts his hat down again.)* I am always willing to be told my own defects, Mr Valentine, by my friends, even when they are as absurdly mistaken about me as you are. I have many faults — very serious faults — of character and temper; but if there is one thing that I am not, it is what you call a prig. *(She closes her lips trimly and looks steadily and challengingly at him as she sits more collectedly than ever.)*

VALENTINE: *(Returning to the end of the garden seat to confront her more emphatically.)* Oh yes, you are. My reason tells me so: my knowledge tells me so: my experience tells me so.

GLORIA: Excuse my reminding you that your reason and your knowledge and your experience are not infallible. At least I hope not.

VALENTINE: I must believe them. Unless you wish me to believe my eyes, my heart, my instincts, my imagination, which are all telling me the most monstrous lies about you.

GLORIA: *(The collectedness beginning to relax.)* Lies!

VALENTINE: *(Obstinately.)* Yes, lies. *(He sits down again beside her.)* Do you expect me to believe that you are the most beautiful woman in the world?

GLORIA: That is ridiculous, and rather personal.

VALENTINE: Of course it's ridiculous. Well, thats what my eyes tell me. *(Gloria makes a movement of contemptuous protest.)* No: I'm not flattering. I tell you I dont believe it. *(She is ashamed to find that this does not quite please her either.)* Do you think that if you were to turn away in disgust from my weakness, I should sit down here and cry like a child?

GLORIA: *(Beginning to find that she must speak shortly and pointedly to keep her voice steady.)* Why should you, pray?

VALENTINE: Of course not: I'm not such an idiot. And yet my heart tells me I should: my fool of a heart. But I'll argue with my heart and bring it to reason. If I loved you a thousand times, I'll force myself to look the truth steadily in the face. After all it's easy to be sensible: the facts are the facts. Whats this place? it's not heaven: it's the Marine Hotel. Whats the time? it's not eternity: it's about half past one in the afternoon. What am I? a dentist: a five shilling dentist!

GLORIA: And I am a feminine prig.

VALENTINE: *(Passionately.)* No, no: I cant face that: I must have one illusion left: the illusion about you. I love you. *(He turns towards her as if the impulse to touch her were ungovernable: she rises and stands on her guard wrathfully. He springs up impatiently and retreats a step.)* Oh, what a fool I am! an idiot! You dont understand: I might as well talk to the stones on the beach. *(He turns away, discouraged.)*

GLORIA: *(Reassured by his withdrawal, and a little remorseful.)* I am sorry. I do not mean to be unsympathetic, Mr Valentine; but what can I say?

VALENTINE: *(Returning to her with all his recklessness of manner replaced by an engaging and chivalrous respect.)* You can say nothing, Miss Clandon. I beg your pardon: it was my own fault, or rather my own bad luck. You see, it all depended on your naturally liking me. *(She is about to speak: he stops her deprecatingly.)* Oh, I know you mustnt tell me whether you like me or not; but —

GLORIA: *(Her principles up in arms at once.)* Must not! Why not? I am a free woman: why should I not tell you?

VALENTINE: *(Pleading in terror, and retreating.)* Dont. I'm afraid to hear.

GLORIA: *(No longer scornful.)* You need not be afraid. I think you are sentimental, and a little foolish; but I like you.

VALENTINE: *(Dropping into the nearest chair as if crushed.)* Then it's all over. *(He becomes the picture of despair.)*

GLORIA: *(Puzzled, approaching him.)* But why?

VALENTINE: Because liking is not enough. Now that I think down into it seriously, I dont know whether I like you or not.

GLORIA: *(Looking down at him with wondering concern.)* I'm sorry.

VALENTINE: *(In an agony of restrained passion.)* Oh, dont pity me. Your voice is tearing my heart to pieces. Let me alone, Gloria. You go down into the very depths of me, troubling and stirring me. I cant struggle with it. I cant tell you —

GLORIA: *(Breaking down suddenly.)* Oh, stop telling me what you feel: I cant bear it.

VALENTINE: *(Springing up triumphantly, the agonized voice now solid, ringing, jubilant.)* Ah, it's come at last: my moment of courage. *(He seizes her hands: she looks at him in terror.)* Our moment of courage! *(He draws her to him; kisses her with impetuous strength; and laughs boyishly.)* Now youve done it, Gloria. It's all over: we're in love with one another. *(She can only gasp at him.)* But what a dragon you were! And how hideously afraid I was!

Antigone

by Jean Anouilh
adapted by Lewis Galantiere

The Play

Please refer to synopsis for this play on page 127.

The Scene

Antigone has risen early to bury her brother. She is confronted by Ismene (her sister) as she returns to her room.

ISMENE: *(Moves to above Center of table.)* Aren't you well?

ANTIGONE: Yes, of course, just a little tired. Because I got up too early. (ANTIGONE *goes to chair Right and sits, suddenly tired.)*

ISMENE: *(Moves to upper Right end of table.)* I couldn't sleep, either.

ANTIGONE: Ismene, you ought not to go without your beauty sleep.

ISMENE: Don't make fun of me.

ANTIGONE: I'm not, truly. This particular morning, seeing how beautiful you are makes everything easier for me. Oh, wasn't I a nasty little beast when we were small? *(She takes* ISMENE*'s hand in hers.)* I used to fling mud at you, and put worms down your neck. I can remember tying you to a tree and cutting off your hair. Your beautiful hair! *(She rises and strokes* ISMENE*'s hair.)* How easy it must be never to be unreasonable with all that smooth silken hair so beautifully set around your head.

ISMENE: *(Takes* ANTIGONE*'s hand in hers.)* Why do you insist upon talking about other things?

ANTIGONE: I am not talking about other things.

ISMENE: Antigone, I've thought about it a lot.

ANTIGONE: Did you?

ISMENE: I thought about it all night long. Antigone, you're mad.

ANTIGONE: Am I?

ISMENE: We cannot do it.

ANTIGONE: Why not?

ISMENE: Creon will have us put to death.

ANTIGONE: Of course he will. But we are *bound* to go out and bury our brother. That's the way it is. What do you think *we* can do to change it?

ISMENE: *(Releases* ANTIGONE*'s hand; draws back a step.)* I don't want to die.

ANTIGONE: I'd prefer not to die, myself. *(*ANTIGONE *crosses below the table over to front of upstage part of arch Left; faces toward the arch.)*

ISMENE: *(Backs away a few steps Right as she turns to* ANTIGONE.*)* Listen to me, Antigone. I thought about it all night. I may be younger than you are, but I always think things over, and you don't.

ANTIGONE: Sometimes it is better *not* to think too much.

ISMENE: I don't agree with you! *(*ISMENE *moves to upper Right end of table and leans on end of table top, toward* ANTIGONE.*)* Oh, I know it's horrible. I *know* Polynices was cheated out of his rights. That he made war — that Creon took sides against him, and he was killed. And I pity Polynices just as much as you do. But all the same, I sort of see what Uncle Creon means. Uncle Creon is the *king* now. He *has* to set an example!

ANTIGONE: *(Turns to* ISMENE.*)* Example! Creon orders that our brother rot and putrefy, and be mangled by dogs and birds of prey. That's an offense against every decent human instinct; against the laws of God and Man. And you talk about examples!

ISMENE: There you go, off on your own again — refusing to pay the slightest heed to anybody. At least you might try to understand!

ANTIGONE: I only understand that a man lies rotting, unburied. And that he is my brother, *(She moves to chair L. of the table.)* and that he must be buried.

ISMENE: But Creon won't let us bury him. And he is stronger than we are. He is the king. He has made himself King.

ANTIGONE: *(Sits.)* I am not listening to you.

ISMENE: *(Kneels on stool, facing toward* ANTIGONE.*)* You *must!*
You know how Creon works. His mob will come running, howling as it runs. A thousand arms will seize our arms. A thousand
breaths will breathe into our faces. Like one single pair of eyes, a
thousand eyes will stare at us. We'll be driven in a tumbril
through their hatred, through the smell of them and their cruel
roaring laughter. We'll be dragged to the scaffold for torture, sur-
rounded by guards with their idiot faces all bloated, their animal
hands clean-washed for the sacrifice, their beefy eyes squinting as
they stare at us. And we'll know that no shrieking and no begging
will make them understand that we want to live, for they are like
trained beasts who go through the motions they've been taught,
without caring about right or wrong. And we shall suffer, we shall
feel pain rising in us until it becomes so unbearable that we *know*
it must stop: but it won't stop: it will go on rising and rising, like a
screaming voice — (ANTIGONE *suddenly sits erect.* ISMENE
sinks down onto the stool, buries her face in her hands and sobs.)
Oh, I can't, I can't, Antigone!
(A pause.)
ANTIGONE: How well you have thought it all out.
ISMENE: I thought of it all night long. Didn't you?
ANTIGONE: Oh, yes.
ISMENE: I'm an awful coward, Antigone.
ANTIGONE: So am I. But what has that to do with it?
ISMENE: *(Raises her head; stares at* ANTIGONE.*)* But Antigone!
Don't you *want* to go on living?
ANTIGONE: Go on living! Who was always the first out of bed every
morning because she loved the touch of the cold morning air on
her bare skin? *(She rises; goes to Left of* ISMENE.*)* Or the last to
bed because nothing less than infinite weariness could wean her
from the lingering night?
ISMENE: *(Clasps* ANTIGONE's *hands, in a sudden rush of tender-
ness.)* Antigone! My darling sister!
ANTIGONE: *(Repulsing her.)* No! For pity's sakes! Don't! *(A pause
as she crosses behind* ISMENE *to upstage Right Center, just below bottom step.)* You say you've thought it all out. The howling
mob: the torture: the fear of death: *(She turns to* ISMENE.*)*
they've made up your mind for you. Is that it?
ISMENE: Yes.
ANTIGONE: *All right.* They're as good excuses as any. (ANTIGONE
moves down to Right of ISMENE *and stands facing Right.)*

ISMENE: *(Turns to* ANTIGONE.*)* Antigone, be reasonable. It's all very well for *men* to believe in ideas, and die for them. But you are a *girl!* Antigone, you have everything in the world to make you happy. All you have to do is — reach out for it. *(She clasps* ANTIGONE's *left hand in hers.)* You are going to be married; you are young; you are beautiful —

ANTIGONE: *(Turns to* ISMENE.*)* I am *not* beautiful.

ISMENE: Oh, yes, you are! Not the way other girls are! But it's always you that the little tough boys turn to look back at when they pass us in the street. And when you go by, the little girls stop talking: they stare and stare at you, until we've turned a corner.

ANTIGONE: *(A faint smile in the corner of her mouth.)* "Little tough boys — little girls."

ISMENE: And what about Haemon?

(A pause.)

ANTIGONE: *(Looks off toward Right.)* I shall see Haemon this morning. I'll take care of Haemon. Go back to bed now, Ismene. The sun is coming up! *(She releases* ISMENE's *hand; crosses behind* ISMENE *to upstage Left Center.)* and as you can see, there is nothing I can do today. Our brother Polynices is as well guarded as if he had won the war and were sitting on his throne.

ISMENE: *(Turns to her.)* What are you going to do?

(The LIGHTING slowly dims up to a higher mark.)

NURSE: *(Calls from offstage Left through arch.)*

Come, my dove. Come to your breakfast.

*(*ANTIGONE *and* ISMENE *glance off in the direction whence came the* NURSE's *voice.)*

ANTIGONE: Please go back to bed.

ISMENE: *(Rises, goes to Right of* ANTIGONE, *and grasps her by the arms.)* If I do — promise me you won't leave the house?

ANTIGONE: *(Takes* ISMENE's *hands in hers.)* Very well, then — I promise. *(*ANTIGONE *releases* ISMENE's *hands, then* ISMENE *goes to arch Left and exits.* ANTIGONE *moves down to chair at Left end of the table.)*

The Importance of Being Earnest
by Oscar Wilde

The Play

Please refer to synopsis for this play on page 136.

The Scene

Gwendolen, engaged to Jack (whom she thinks is Ernest), makes a call on her betrothed's ward, Cecily. Discovering that Cecily is very pretty, Gwendolen wants to make sure that Cecily is no more than a ward to her betrothed. Cecily, assuring her not to worry, announces her engagement to Ernest. Gwendolen, also thinking that she is engaged to Ernest, cites a prior claim. A delightful, Victorian catfight ensues.

CECILY: *(Advancing to meet her.)* Pray let me introduce myself to you. My name is Cecily Cardew.

GWENDOLEN: Cecily Cardew? *(Moving to her and shaking hands.)* What a very sweet name! Something tells me that we are going to be great friends. I like you already more than I can say. My first impressions of people are never wrong.

CECILY: How nice of you to like me so much after we have known each other such a comparatively short time. Pray sit down

GWENDOLEN: *(Still standing up.)* I may call you Cecily, may I not?

CECILY: With pleasure!

GWENDOLEN: And you will always call me Gwendolen, won't you?

CECILY: If you wish.

CECILY: I hope so. *(A pause. They both sit down together.)*

GWENDOLEN: Then that is all quite settled, is it not?

GWENDOLEN: Perhaps this might be a favorable opportunity for my mentioning who I am. My father is Lord Bracknell. You have heard of Papa, I suppose?

CECILY: I don't think so.

GWENDOLEN: Outside the family circle, Papa, I am glad to say, is entirely unknown. I think that is quite as it should be. The home seems to me to be the proper sphere for the man. And certainly once a man begins to neglect his domestic duties he becomes painfully effeminate, does he not? And I don't like that. It makes men so very attractive. Cecily, Mamma, whose views on education are remarkably strict, has brought me up to be extremely short-sighted; it is part of her system; so do you mind my looking at you through my glasses?

CECILY: Oh! Not at all, Gwendolen. I am very fond of being looked at.

GWENDOLEN: *(After examining* CECILY *carefully through a lorgnette.)* You are here on a short visit, I suppose.

CECILY: Oh, no! I live here.

GWENDOLEN: *(Severely.)* Really? Your mother, no doubt, or some female relative of advanced years, resides here also?

CECILY: Oh, no! I have no mother, nor, in fact any relations.

GWENDOLEN: Indeed?

CECILY: My dear guardian, with the assistance of Miss Prism, has the arduous task of looking after me.

GWENDOLEN: Your guardian?

CECILY: Yes, I am Mr. Worthing's ward.

GWENDOLEN: Oh! It is strange he never mentioned to me that he had a ward. How secretive of him! He grows more interesting hourly. I am not sure, however, that the news inspires me with feelings of unmixed delight. *(Rising and going to* CECILY*.)* I am very fond of you, Cecily; I have liked you ever since I met you! But I am bound to state that now that I know that you are Mr. Worthing's ward, I cannot help expressing a wish you were — well just a little older than you seem to be — and not quite so very alluring in appearance. In fact, if I may speak candidly —

CECILY: Pray do! I think that whenever one has anything unpleasant to say, one should always be quite candid.

GWENDOLEN: Well, to speak with perfect candor, Cecily, I wish that you were fully forty-two, and more than usually plain for your age. Ernest has a strong upright nature. He is the very soul of truth and honor. Disloyalty would be as impossible to him as deception. But even men of the noblest possible moral character are extremely susceptible to the influence of the physical charms of others. Modern, no less than ancient history, supplies us with many most painful examples of what I refer to. If it were not so, indeed, history would be quite unreadable.

CECILY: I beg your pardon, Gwendolen, did you say Ernest?

GWENDOLEN: Yes.

CECILY: Oh, but it is not Mr. Ernest Worthing who is my guardian. It is his brother — his elder brother.

GWENDOLEN: *(Sitting down again.)* Ernest never mentioned to me that he had a brother.

CECILY: I am sorry to say they have not been on good terms for a long time.

GWENDOLEN: Ah! That accounts for it. And now that I think of it I have never heard any man mention his brother. The subject seems distasteful to most men. Cecily, you have lifted a load from my mind. I was growing almost anxious. It would have been terrible if any cloud had come across a friendship like ours, would it not? Of course you are quite, quite sure that it is not Mr. Ernest Worthing who is your guardian?

CECILY: Quite sure. *(A pause.)* In fact, I am going to be his.

GWENDOLEN: *(Enquiringly.)* I beg your pardon?

CECILY: *(Rather shy and confidingly.)* Dearest Gwendolen, there is no reason why I should make a secret of it to you. Our little county newspaper is sure to chronicle the fact next week. Mr. Ernest Worthing and I are engaged to be married.

GWENDOLEN: *(Quite politely, rising.)* My darling Cecily, I think there must be some slight error. Mr. Ernest Worthing is engaged to me. The announcement will appear in the *Morning Post* on Saturday at the latest.

CECILY: *(Very politely, rising.)* I am afraid you must be under some misconception. Ernest proposed to me exactly ten minutes ago. *(Shows diary.)*

GWENDOLEN: *(Examining diary through her lorgnette carefully.)* It is certainly very curious, for he asked me to be his wife yesterday afternoon at five-thirty. If you would care to verify the incident, pray do so. *(Produces a diary of her own.)* I never travel without my diary. One should always have something sensational to read in the train. I am so sorry, dear Cecily, if it is any disappointment to you, but I am afraid *I* have the prior claim.

CECILY: It would distress me more than I can tell you, dear Gwendolen, if it caused you any mental or physical anguish, but I feel bound to point out that since Ernest proposed to you he clearly has changed his mind.

GWENDOLEN: *(Meditatively.)* If the poor fellow has been entrapped into any foolish promise I shall consider it my duty to rescue him at once, and with a firm hand.

CECILY: *(Thoughtfully and sadly.)* Whatever unfortunate entanglement my dear boy may have got into, I will never reproach him with it after we are married.

GWENDOLEN: Do you allude to me, Miss Cardew, as an entanglement? You are presumptuous. On an occasion of this kind it becomes more than a moral duty to speak one's mind. It becomes a pleasure.

CECILY: Do you suggest, Miss Fairfax, that I entrapped Ernest into an engagement? How dare you? This is no time for wearing the shallow mask of manners. When I see a spade, I call it a spade.

GWENDOLEN: *(Satirically.)* I am glad to say that I have never seen a spade. It is obvious that our social spheres have been widely different.

(Enter MERRIMAN, *followed by the footman. He carries a salver, table cloth, and plate stand.* CECILY *is about to retort. The presence of the servants exercises a restraining influence, under which both girls chafe.)*

MERRIMAN: Shall I lay tea here as usual, Miss?

CECILY: *(Sternly, in a calm voice.)* Yes, as usual. *(*MERRIMAN *begins to clear and lay cloth. A long pause.* CECILY *and* GWENDOLEN *glare at each other.)*

GWENDOLEN: Are there many interesting walks in the vicinity, Miss Cardew?

CECILY: Oh yes! a great many. From the top of one of the hills quite close one can see five counties.

GWENDOLEN: Five counties! I don't think I should like that. I hate crowds.

CECILY: *(Sweetly.)* I suppose that is why you live in town?

GWENDOLEN: *(Bites her lip and beats her foot furiously with her parasol. Looking round.)* Quite a well-kept garden this is, Miss Cardew.

CECILY: So glad you like it, Miss Fairfax.

GWENDOLEN: I had no idea there were any flowers in the country.

CECILY: Oh, flowers are as common here, Miss Fairfax, as people are in London.

GWENDOLEN: Personally I cannot understand how anybody manages to exist in the country, if anybody who is anybody does. The country always bores me to death.

CECILY: Ah! This is what the newspapers call agricultural depression, is it not? I believe the aristocracy are suffering very much from it just at present. It is almost an epidemic amongst them, I have been told. May I offer you some tea, Miss Fairfax?

GWENDOLEN: *(With elaborate politeness.)* Thank you. *(Aside.)* Detestable girl! But I require tea!

CECILY: *(Sweetly.)* Sugar?

GWENDOLEN: *(Superciliously.)* No, thank you. Sugar is not fashionable any more.

CECILY: *(Looks angrily at* GWENDOLEN, *takes up the tongs and puts four lumps of sugar into the cup. Severely.)* Cake or bread and butter?

GWENDOLEN: *(In a bored manner.)* Bread and butter, please. Cake is rarely seen at the best houses nowadays.

CECILY: *(Cuts a very large slice of cake and puts it on the tray.)* Hand that to Miss Fairfax. *(*MERRIMAN *does so, and goes out with footman.)*

GWENDOLEN: *(Drinks the tea and makes a grimace. Puts down cup at once, reaches out her hand to the bread and butter, looks at it, and finds it is cake. Rises in indignation.)* You have filled my tea with lumps of sugar, and though I asked most distinctly for bread and butter, you have given me cake. I am known for the gentleness of my disposition, and the extraordinary sweetness of my nature, but I warn you, Miss Cardew, you may go too far.

CECILY: *(Rising.)* To save my poor, innocent, trusting boy from the machinations of any other girl there are no lengths to which I would not go.

GWENDOLEN: From the moment I saw you I distrusted you. I felt you were false and deceitful. I am never deceived in such matters. My first impressions of people are invariably right.

CECILY: It seems to me, Miss Fairfax, that I am trespassing on your valuable time. No doubt you have many other calls of a similar character to make in the neighborhood.

(Two Males)

The Importance of Being Earnest
by Oscar Wilde

The Play

Please refer to synopsis for this play on page 136.

The Scene

Jack has proposed marriage to Gwendolen and she has agreed. However, Lady Bracknell is concerned about his family background. Jack was found in a handbag in a railroad station and knows very little about himself. He has been advised by Lady Bracknell to "try and acquire some relations as soon as possible, and to try and make a definite effort to produce at any rate one parent, of either sex before the season is quite over." The scene begins with Jack discussing this situation with his friend, Algernon, the nephew of Lady Bracknell.

ALGERNON: Didn't it go off all right, old boy? You don't mean to say Gwendolen refused you? I know it is a way she has. She is always refusing people. I think it is most ill-natured of her.

JACK: Oh, Gwendolen is as right as a trivet. As far as she is concerned, we are engaged. Her mother is perfectly unbearable. Never met such a Gorgon. . . . I don't really know what a Gorgon is like, but I am quite sure that Lady Bracknell is one. In any case, she is a monster, without being a myth, which is rather unfair. . . . I beg your pardon, Algy, I suppose I shouldn't talk about your own aunt in that way before you.

ALGERNON: My dear boy, I love hearing my relations abused. It is the only thing that makes me put up with them all. Relations are simply a tedious pack of people, who haven't got the remotest knowledge of how to live, nor the smallest instinct about when to die.

JACK: Oh, that is nonsense!

ALGERNON: It isn't!

JACK: Well, I won't argue about the matter. You always want to argue about things.

ALGERNON: That is exactly what things were originally made for.

JACK: Upon my word, if I thought that, I'd shoot myself.... *(A pause.)* You don't think there is any chance of Gwendolen becoming like her mother in about a hundred and fifty years, do you, Algy?

ALGERNON: All women become like their mothers. That is their tragedy. No man does. That's his.

JACK: Is that clever?

ALGERNON: It is perfectly phrased! and quite as true as any observation in civilized life should be.

JACK: I am sick to death of cleverness. Everybody is clever nowadays. You can't go anywhere without meeting clever people. The thing has become an absolute public nuisance. I wish to goodness we had a few fools left.

ALGERNON: We have.

JACK: I should extremely like to meet them. What do they talk about?

ALGERNON: The fools? Oh! about the clever people, of course.

JACK: What fools.

ALGERNON: By the way, did you tell Gwendolen the truth about your being Ernest in town, and Jack in the country?

JACK: *(In a very patronizing manner.)* My dear fellow, the truth isn't quite the sort of thing one tells to a nice, sweet, refined girl. What extraordinary ideas you have about the way to behave to a woman!

ALGERNON: The only way to behave to a woman is to make love to her, if she is pretty, and to someone else, if she is plain.

JACK: Oh, that is nonsense.

ALGERNON: What about your brother? What about the profligate Ernest?

JACK: Oh, before the end of the week I shall have got rid of him. I'll say he died in Paris of apoplexy. Lots of people die of apoplexy, quite suddenly, don't they?

ALGERNON: Yes, but it's hereditary, my dear fellow. It's a sort of thing that runs in families. You had much better say a severe chill.

JACK: You are sure a severe chill isn't hereditary, or anything of that kind?

ALGERNON: Of course it isn't!

JACK: Very well, then. My poor brother Ernest is carried off suddenly, in Paris, by a severe chill. That gets rid of him.

ALGERNON: But I thought you said that . . . Miss Cardew was a little too much interested in your poor brother Ernest? Won't she feel his loss a good deal?

JACK: Oh, that is all right. Cecily is not a silly romantic girl, I am glad to say. She has got a capital appetite, goes long walks, and pays no attention at all to her lessons.

ALGERNON: I would rather like to see Cecily.

JACK: I will take very good care you never do. She is excessively pretty, and she is only just eighteen.

ALGERNON: Have you told Gwendolen yet that you have an excessively pretty ward who is only just eighteen?

JACK: Oh! one doesn't blurt these things out to people. Cecily and Gwendolen are perfectly certain to be extremely great friends. I'll bet you anything you like that half an hour after they have met, they will be calling each other sister.

ALGERNON: Women only do that when they have called each other a lot of other things first. Now, my dear boy, if we want to get a good table at Willis's we really must go and dress. Do you know it is nearly seven?

JACK: *(Irritably.)* Oh! it always is nearly seven.

ALGERNON: Well, I'm hungry.

JACK: I never knew you when you weren't. . . .

ALGERNON: What shall we do after dinner? Go to a theatre?

JACK: Oh, no! I loathe listening.

ALGERNON: Well, let us go to the Club?

JACK: Oh, no! I hate talking.

ALGERNON: Well, we might trot round to the Empire at ten?

JACK: Oh, no! I can't bear looking at things. It is so silly.

ALGERNON: Well, what shall we do?

JACK: Nothing!

ALGERNON: It is awfully hard work doing nothing. However, I don't mind hard work where there is no definite object of any kind.

INDEX
Authors and Play Titles

ABOUT THE EDITOR

Barbara Marchant is the associate head of the B.F.A. acting program at the Mason Gross School of the Arts at Rutgers University. She trained with William Esper as an actress and teacher. Ms. Marchant has appeared on Broadway and daytime television. In regional theater she has been seen in such varied roles as Blanche in *A Streetcar Named Desire*, Corrinna in *House of Blue Leaves*, Isadora Duncan in *U.S.A.*, and in the acclaimed production of *Lenny* at the Charles Playhouse. Some of her New York credits include work at the Manhattan Theater Club, Performance Garage, and Theater for the New City. She performed throughout Europe in the Obie-nominated *Medicine Show*. Recent directorial credits include *The Cover of Life* at the Harper Joy Theater and *Hermie Holler Here* at Manhattan Theater Source. She has taught at The Berkshire Theater Festival, Emory University, Whitman College, the American College Theater Festival sponsored by the Kennedy Center, The Broadway Project sponsored by the University of Tel Aviv, and Theater De Trap in Amsterdam.

Ms. Marchant has been an adjudicator for the University Resident Theater Association's national auditions and was awarded the Rutgers University Teacher of the Year Award. She is the co-founder of the London Academy of Theater (sponsored by Dame Judi Dench) and the chair of their advisory committee. A staff member of the William Esper Studio, she has been on the faculty of the Mason Gross School of the Arts since 1984 and also coaches professionally.